BOOK
ART STUDIO
HANDBOOK

For AMR – Amy, For DLH – Stacie

© 2013 Quarry Books
Text © 2013 Stacie Dolin and Amy Lapidow

First published in the United States of America by
Quarry Books, a member of
Quayside Publishing Group
100 Cummings Center
Suite 406-L
Beverly, Massachusetts 01915-6101
Telephone: (978) 282-9590
Fax: (978) 283-2742
www.quarrybooks.com
Visit www.Craftside.Typepad.com for a behind-the-scenes peek at our crafty world!

Library of Congress Cataloging-in-Publication Data

Dolin, Stacie.
  Book art studio handbook : techniques and methods for binding books, creating albums, making boxes and more / Stacie Dolin and Amy Lapidow.
      pages cm
  Summary: "As the "book" morphs and evolves into a malleable, digital file, interest in the classic form is reignited in book lovers and crafters. The Book Art Studio Handbook offers readers a comprehensive and accessible guide to not only the nuts and bolts of this classic art, but insight into the artisan's lifestyle. This book goes beyond quick craft projects and into the heart of bookmaking, binding, letterpress printing, decorative cover techniques, book conservation, and other book arts. It is an essential companion book for all paper lovers and bibliophiles--especially as the book as object becomes more prominent a concept"-- Provided by publisher.
  ISBN 978-1-59253-818-8 (pbk.)
  1. Bookbinding--Handbooks, manuals, etc. 2. Books--Handbooks, manuals, etc. I. Lapidow, Amy. II. Title.
  Z271.D63 2013
  686.3--dc23
                                                                    2012022313

ISBN: 978-1-59253-818-8

Digital edition published in 2013
eISBN: 978-1-61058-620-7

10 9 8 7 6 5 4 3 2 1

Design: Laura H. Couallier, Laura Herrmann Design
Photography: Glenn Scott Photography
All illustrations by Mattie Reposa with the exception of page 37 by Gayle Isabelle Ford

Printed in China

BOOK
ART STUDIO
HANDBOOK

Techniques and Methods for Binding Books, Creating Albums,
Making Boxes and Enclosures, and More

Stacie Dolin & Amy Lapidow

Quarry Books
100 Cummings Center, Suite 406L
Beverly, MA 01915

quarrybooks.com • craftside.typepad.com

Contents

Friend-of-a-Friend Book,
Stacie Dolin.

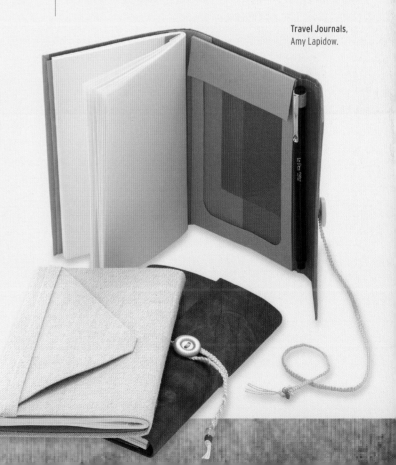

Travel Journals,
Amy Lapidow.

Introduction

Welcome to *Book Art Studio Handbook*! This primer covers the fundamentals of creating books and related objects by hand. Basic tools and materials are described, as well as the essential techniques and concepts to use them effectively.

This guide will show you that you can create interesting work with minimal equipment, a little bit of time, and a dose of imagination. We will teach you the skills you need to make beautiful, structurally sound books to house photographs, writing, illustrations, and much more. You can easily alter the structures we describe to accommodate a variety of content. And all of the books featured in this primer are easy to make without the use of large equipment.

While making the projects, refer to the introductory sections on materials, tools, and techniques to become adept in their use. Understanding the materials on hand and accommodating them accordingly will minimize later problems with the structures. Having the right tools

for the job will make things much easier, and will aid in your mastery of the techniques and fine hand skills described; practice using these things together in order to hone your fine hand skills.

Each section is fully illustrated to enhance the step-by-step instructions. Look at the tip boxes for extra pieces of advice. The gallery photos at the beginning of each project will show you variations to spur ideas. Mix, match, and combine ideas or techniques from one project to another. Be patient and have fun!

Additional pieces in the gallery pages will inspire you with ideas of what you can do with these techniques. Experiment with materials that inspire you and make the book your own.

Have fun! Make books!
– Stacie and Amy

Some book artists use a sewing frame to keep tapes taut, but it isn't necessary.

Getting
Started

CHAPTER

1

Planning
Your Studio

Welcome to your book art studio! Before you get started, consider where you will work and gather the supplies you will use regularly. Having everything in place will set the stage for many happy hours of bookbinding experimentation.

The following sections will give you an overview of how to create your workspace, what materials you should have on hand, the basic tools you will need, and how to use them. The information we provide here encompasses the fundamentals that are used in every project no matter how advanced the bookbinder's skills. As your skills expand, the types of materials you use can expand as well, and you can add more specialized equipment.

Keep a variety of both handmade and commercial decorative papers on hand to personalize your books.

Create Your Workspace

It is important to have a clean, dedicated, well-lit workspace. A sturdy countertop is perfect, as many things are done while standing, and working at a table while standing can lead to back and wrist pain. There are varying opinions as to what is a good height for a working table. The average is waist height or where your hands can work easily with your elbows bent. We tend to do everything standing, except sewing, so the task is in complete view from above. Experiment and see what is the most comfortable for you. An ample amount of overhead and/or natural light is best, while an adjustable task lamp can be useful when working on more detailed projects.

You can scale your workspace to the space you have. We know bookbinders who work in large studios and bookbinders who work in a dedicated corner of their kitchen.

Having things easily accessible is important as well. It's frustrating to not have an extra piece of waste paper on hand when gluing things up, for example, and having to look for press boards while things are drying can cause warping. Label boxes and folders so that you can find things easily. Art bins or organizational products that are easily found in craft stores work very well.

BASIC SUPPLIES

Here are a few of the consumable supplies you'll be choosing for each project in this book. Most can be found at general art stores, or at the specialty suppliers in the back of this book (see Resources on page 152).

PAPER

Paper is measured by weight, in either pounds or grams. As you work with your favorite papers, it will become easier for you to tell what works best. Think about the project and what would be the best characteristics to have in the paper.

Is it text paper or for the cover? Should it be able to fold? Is it good for writing in ink, pencil, or fountain pen? Choose paper that suits the book's needs. Is longevity an issue? Look for something that is archival so that it will not degrade or have an adverse effect on the items within. A medium-weight paper might be best. Are you making a sketchbook? Try watercolor paper. Text paper around 70 lb. text (measured by pounds per ream or 500 sheets)/90 gsm (grams per square meter, the actual weight of the sheet) for the interior of the book, or text block, is a good all-around paper weight. We use Mohawk Superfine 70 lb. text (104 gsm) for most textblock paper.

For cover papers, keep a variety of decorative papers on hand. These should also be able to fold and should not crack or break. Very thick paper might be hard to glue down, and papers that are too light allow the glue to come through and stain. Try a medium-weight paper to start. Canson Mi-Teintes is a good all-around paper that comes in many colors and is easy to find.

There are so many patterns available in decorated papers that there is something for everyone. Some even have inclusions—bits of things like flowers or colored fibers embedded in them. Papers also come from every part of the world. It is fun just to look at all the possibilities and imagine what you can make with them. In the beginning, try not to get paper that will be difficult to handle when glue is applied. They are very pretty and hard to resist, but since they are *very* lightweight they turn into something like a wet paper towel once glue is brushed on.

Keep a variety of undecorated colored papers around as well. It is nice to have a solid color to complement something decorated. A medium weight is the most versatile.

The best way to choose a paper is to go to the store and touch it. Will it do what you need it to do for the project?

And finally, stock up on waste paper: newsprint, old photocopy/printer paper, and the like. Use it to glue on, so as not to make a mess in your work area.

BOARD

Most board is labeled as archival, which is good in terms of longevity. If it is not labeled archival or acid-free, assume it is not. Consider the project to decide whether something that is not archival is appropriate. Board is measured using the point system; each point is one one-thousandth of an inch. In binder's board, a thin board would be listed as .067 or .070 pt. A thick board would be more like .098 pt.

The projects in this book use these boards:

- .040 pt. or 4-ply mat board (easy to find, comes in a variety of colors, and nice on thinner books)
- .070 pt. board (light binder's board with a good all-around thickness)
- .010 pt. board (folder stock)
- .020 pt. board (2-ply or card stock)

BOOK CLOTH

Book cloth is either starched, so it's forgiving and easy to work with, or it can be backed with paper, which means it's easily stained but very good looking. It is also possible to make book cloth from regular fabric and to back it with a Japanese paper or iron-on fusible interfacing.

ADHESIVES

You have two primary options for glue: PVA (polyvinyl acetate) and wheat paste. PVA is a white glue that dries clear. It's acid-free, and it *stains*. It will come off tools, but not the book or your clothing. (The reversible type does come out of clothes.)

Wheat paste, which you can get in instant or cooked form, dries clear, does not stain, and is reversible with water. It is slow to dry.

You will also need some double-sided tape.

THREAD

Unwaxed linen sewing thread, which you will see in many projects, is measured by the number of strands that make up the cord and the number of twists per inch. The larger the number, the more twists, and the

Book cloth is starched or paper-backed and ideal for bookmaking, and available in a variety of colors and patterns.

thinner the thread. A thread made up of two strands or regular sewing thread is not strong enough for bookbinding. The projects in this book use these threads:

- 25/3 (three strands, twisted 25 times per inch; a medium-thin thread)
- 18/3 (three strands, twisted 18 times per inch; a thicker thread)

OTHER SUPPLIES

Other supplies used in the projects in this book include hemp or linen cord, beads, buttons, Velcro buttons, and ribbon. Be creative!

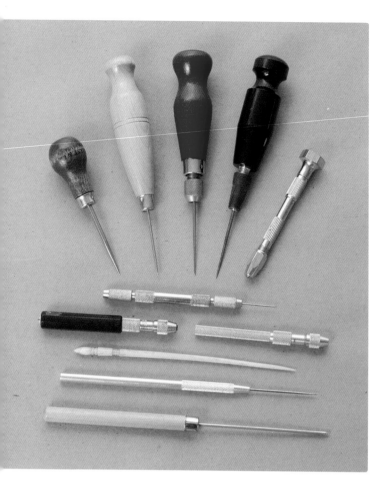

A selection of awls, most often used for punching holes

BOOKBINDING AWL, CERAMICS NEEDLE TOOL, OR PIN VISE

You can use your bookbinding awl to punch sewing stations into a textblock. You can also use it as a marking tool. Choose something thin and tapered, and with a sturdy point. The point can often be adjusted or changed on these tools depending on how you will use them.

BEESWAX

Beeswax is used on thread to discourage it from fraying, twisting, and knotting. It is also used to create a sheen and to smooth out hand-decorated papers when burnished with a bone folder. To wax a piece of thread in preparation for sewing, run the thread over the beeswax once or twice, sliding it under your thumb while pressing it to the wax. Microcrystaline, a synthetic wax, can also be used.

Basic Equipment to Have on Hand

Here are some of the tools you'll need to get started. Keeping these tools in stock and organized is the first step toward creating professional-quality books.

APRON

Some bookbinding techniques can get messy, and as mentioned earlier, PVA glue does not come out of clothing. A bib-front apron will ensure that your clothing does not get dirty. And an apron pocket is useful for tucking away frequently used tools so that they do not get lost on your workbench.

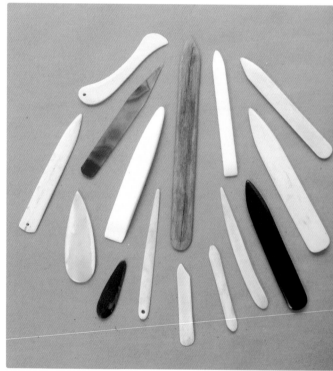

There are a variety of bone folders available—find the one that's right for you!

BONE FOLDER

Bone folders are made of cow bone, though you can also find versions made of antler, agate, or horn. Teflon folders are also available, and they are more flexible than the aforementioned types. Bone folders are used for many purposes, such as scoring a fold, making a crease, or folding paper over a board edge. Your bone folder will become almost an extension of your hand. Modify a real bone folder with wet/dry sandpaper to make a sharper point or a creasing edge as desired.

TIP	**Modify Your Bone Folder**

To give your bone folder a sharper point or edge, which will allow it to make sharper creases, we recommend that you modify it using wet/dry sandpaper. Align the edge of the folder to your sandpaper and drag it toward you in a smooth motion, as shown here. *Do not* modify a Teflon folder with sandpaper. Those can be carved to a desired shape instead.

Keep a variety of glue and paste brushes on hand so that you always have the size and type you need.

BRUSHES

It is good to have a variety of glue and paste brushes in assorted sizes: round, flat, big, and small. Use the largest brush possible in comparison to the size of the item you're gluing; that way the glue will not have dried by the time you have covered the surface of the item with adhesive. Use a synthetic brush for synthetic adhesives and a natural brush for natural adhesives.

Keep the brushes very clean or they will not last very long. Brush soap is available at art stores; it nourishes the bristles. However, any mild soap will work. Keep the brushes in use in a jar or glass with water just up to the top of the bristles. To prevent spills and drips from getting on your work, put the water jar in a cake tin or on a tray.

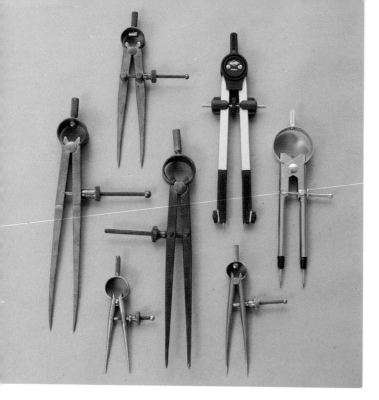

A collection of dividers for measuring and marking

DIVIDERS

Dividers are useful for measuring without a ruler. You can also use them as marking tools.

ERASERS

Pink Pearl or white vinyl erasers are good general-use erasers. If you're erasing on black paper, consider using a black eraser so that there are no streaks. Always use erasers with care on fragile papers, as they may cause pilling or streaking. And always test your erasers on a waste piece of the paper you will be using them on. Stroke your eraser from the inside, not up and down.

FENCES

Fences are moisture barriers that you can put between anything that has been glued and the rest of the book—for example, between a cover and the textblock, or between pages. A fence is necessary so that after gluing or pasting, the rest of the book does not get wet and warp because moisture was introduced

to it. Just slide a piece of .010 or .020 pt. board (light board or folder stock) between what was glued and what should be kept dry. Let the item sit under a weight with the fence in it until it is dry. Waxed paper or butcher's paper can also be used.

GLUE CONTAINER

Use a plastic or glass container with a tight-fitting lid to store small amounts of glue dispensed from a larger container. For screw lids, put a layer of waxed paper on top of the container before putting on the lid. When the glue is used up, leave the container open to let the remaining bits of glue air-dry. The dried glue will then peel off the container.

HAND DRILL

A hand drill is not used often, but it is helpful for drilling through board, or through a large stack of paper.

MAT KNIVES

You'll need both big and small knives. We favor Olfa brand knives because each blade has multiple segments, so you can break off the top segment to form a new edge. You should do this quite often, as a sharp blade is much more efficient than a dull one. Also, these knives have a flat profile, so the handle does not get in the way of cutting, thereby skewing your measurements. We also recommend X-Acto brand knives, which are easier to manipulate when doing delicate work or cutting curves.

PENCIL

A mechanical pencil is best, as it is always sharp. Mark lightly so that the lines are easy to erase.

RULERS

You will use your ruler as a measuring device, and as a straightedge along which to make cuts. It should be rather rigid. Get a ruler without cork backing. Although cork backing may be a useful slip guard, the point of the knife can slip underneath the gap between the metal and the paper, skewing your cuts.

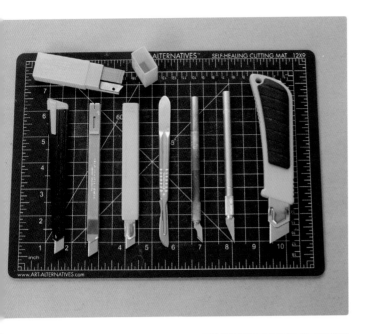

When choosing a ruler, get one that has the increment lines engraved; that way, if the ink wears off, the ruler is still usable. Also, make sure the measurement starts at the end of the ruler. It becomes confusing very quickly when the increments are inset.

The metric system is easier to use in the long term than the imperial system. Although it might seem confusing at first if you aren't familiar with it, the metric system is really as easy as counting up to ten. There are ten millimeters in one centimeter. The small increment lines are millimeters; the large ones are centimeters. The measurements provided for the projects are not exact conversions between metric and imperial. We have provided numbers that make sense.

NEEDLES

Stock up on #8 milliner's or #18 sharp bookbinder's needles; they have large eyes and can fit the most common bookbinding threads. Crewel or sharps can also be used. Look for needles with an eye that is close to the size of the shaft of the needle.

90-DEGREE TRIANGLE

Make sure your triangle has a cutting edge and a grid. This is a great tool to use to align and cut papers, while making sure everything is square.

PAPER TOWELS

Keeping everything clean is a constant challenge. You can use a damp paper towel or cloth that you won't mind getting messy to wipe off sticky fingers.

PRESS BOARDS

Press boards are used with a weight to keep items flat while drying. Make your press boards out of plywood, and cut them into either rectangles or squares, that are larger than the item you are making; 12" × 12" (30.5 × 30.5 cm) and 12" × 14" (30.5 × 35.5 cm) are useful sizes. Line your press boards with clean, smooth binder's board and masking tape. Replace your press boards whenever they get messy. They are for pressing only; do not cut on them, because any cut mark on the lining will emboss on the work you press.

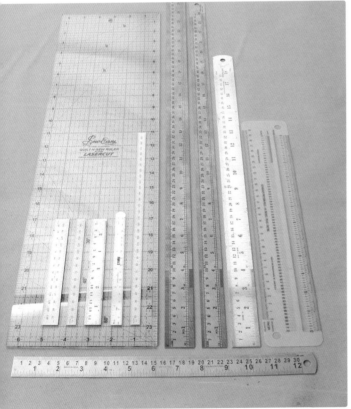

ABOVE TOP Stock both large and small knives.

ABOVE BOTTOM An assortment of rulers of different lengths and widths

Line Your Press Boards

To line your press boards, measure the wood dimensions directly on the binder's board, and cut the binder's board to those dimensions (1). The binder's board should go to the edges of the plywood. Use masking tape along the edges to adhere the binder's board to the press board (2).

RUBBER CEMENT PICKUP/CREPE SQUARE

Use a rubber cement pickup—also called a crepe square—to clean up your work. When used carefully, it can pick up errant spots of dried glue.

SANDPAPER

Use sandpaper with a fine grit (220 or higher) to smooth out any rough edges on your binder's boards. A piece of sandpaper mounted on a scrap piece of binder's board is useful for sanding the edges of boards without rounding them. You can use wet/dry sandpaper to modify bone folders. Sanding sticks and other holders come in handy when working on smaller things.

SCISSORS

Your scissors should be very sharp and should cut right to the point. Having pairs of both large and small scissors is convenient for working with different materials and different sizes. It is worth investing in a good pair of scissors that are only for use on paper and bookbinding. They should fit comfortably in your hand.

SELF-HEALING CUTTING MAT OR SCRAP BOARD

Cut on a cutting mat or on a piece of scrap binder's board that you don't mind marking up with cuts and nicks. This helps to keep your work area clean. If you're using scrap board, replace it often so that old cuts and nicks do not interfere with the current project.

SEWING TAPES

Many books are sewn on a support system, either tapes or cord. In this book, the supports are linen sewing tapes. The textblock is attached to the tapes with the sewing. The supports give the sewing something to hold on to, to give the structure stability.

Sewing tapes come in a variety of widths. The projects in this book use a ¼" (7 mm)-wide tape. It is made of linen and is very strong. It can be purchased through the suppliers at the back of the book (see Resources on page 152).

COMFORTABLE SHOES

Wear good, comfortable shoes. Most bookbinding techniques are performed while standing up. Standing gives the best view of the work (i.e., straight down), so everything remains square.

WATER JAR

Be sure to fill your water jar only until the water reaches the top of the brush bristles so that the ferrule—the piece of metal that holds the bristles to the shaft—does not rust. Make sure the jar is not easily tipped over.

WAXED PAPER

Put waxed paper next to or between anything that might be messy and stick when pressed.

An array of possible weights. Note that the brick weights are covered with fabric.

WEIGHTS

You will need to weigh down your projects to press them. Any heavy object will work: bricks covered in heavy paper or cloth, old lead type, food cans, antique irons, and so on. Tins filled with buckshot or pennies make good small weights. Use your weights in combination with a press board.

Diving weights work well, and they come in different sizes. Belt weights are solid; vest weights are sold in bags. If they are not covered with something, cover them, as they are made of lead. Significant exposure to lead is harmful. As a general practice, any lead should be covered so that it can be handled safely. Even though the exposure here is very limited, cover it up and wash your hands after you touch any exposed lead.

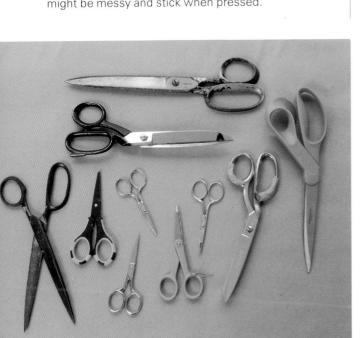

Start with a pair of large and a pair of small scissors, and make sure they fit comfortably in your hand.

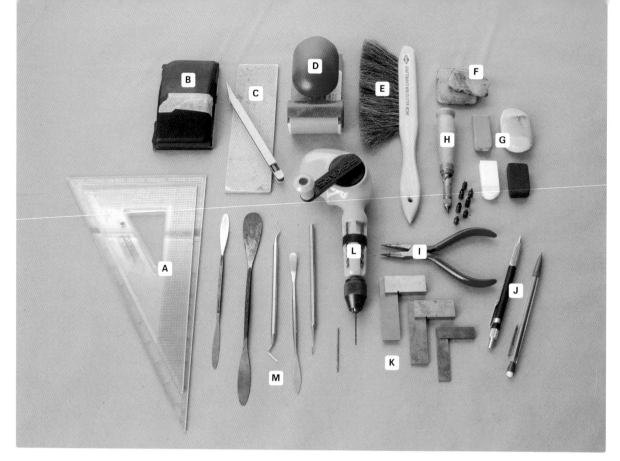

Tools and Equipment That Are Nice to Have

Here are some tools that aren't necessary to get started, but are nice to have. Consider investing in them as you become more experienced at bookbinding and you know what you will use, and what will make your projects easier.

PUNCHING TROUGH

A punching trough holds the sections while you're punching sewing stations and ensures that the holes will be properly aligned. It is easy to make one out of scrap board. It will not last forever, so use it until it falls apart and then make another one. You can also punch sections using an open phone book to steady the paper, or on a scrap board on your table. See page 22 for how to make one.

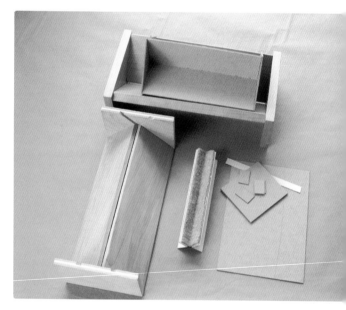

A selection of punching troughs

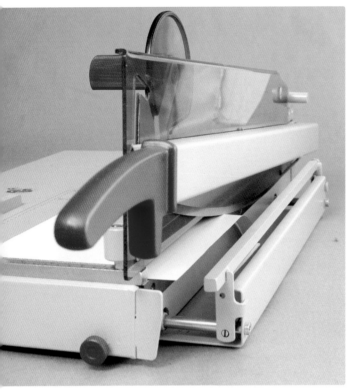

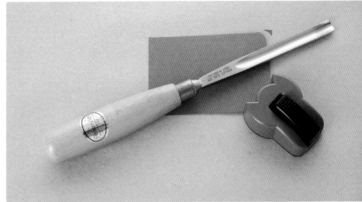

NIPPING PRESS

A nipping press is useful for pressing paper and for making sure that something you have glued is actually adhered. (See photo, page 43.) Nipping presses come in different sizes and with varying amounts of "daylight" (the amount of space between the platens). The platens are the flat plates that move up and down to press down on the objects between. Choose one that will accommodate the most items you might use. Use extra press boards to fill out the daylight for smaller books.

PAPER CUTTER

Office-type paper cutters are not well suited to book-binding. They tend to lack the strength necessary to accurately cut the materials, and they tend to "pull" the paper with the blade, giving inaccurate cuts. We recommend Kutrimmer paper cutters, which are sized for home use and can accurately cut both paper and board. They have a fixed clamp to hold the paper in place and keep it from pulling.

MICROSPATULA

A microspatula, also called a *Casselli spatula*, is very useful for getting into small spaces.

CORNER ROUNDER

A corner rounder is useful for consistently rounding the corners of many pages at once. You can find corner rounders in the rubber-stamping tools section of your supplies store. They are used for paper only. A round chisel can also be used, and it is suitable for use on binder's board.

MACHINIST'S SQUARE

You can use a machinist's square to jog sections against while sewing. You can also use it to transfer measurements to covers and spines.

TEFLON FOLDER

See the earlier section on bone folders for more information.

Making a Punching Trough

A punching trough is key to lining up your textblock accurately. It's also easy to make—and good thing, because you'll make it again when it wears out!

MATERIALS

- 1 piece of binder's board for the trough (about 8" × 10" [20 × 25 cm] for the projects in this book)
- 2 square pieces of binder's board for the ends, with the height and width the same as half the width of the trough piece (4" [10 cm])
- 4 small pieces of binder's board for the braces, cut to ½" × 1" (1.5 × 2.5 cm)
- 1 piece of cord the length of the trough (optional)
- Knife
- Ruler/straightedge
- Glue

Instructions

1. Determine the center of the trough. Try using a piece of paper the width of the trough piece, and folding the paper in half.

2. Mark the halfway point at two places on the trough piece.

3. Align the ruler/straightedge to the marks.

4. Make several cuts with the knife along the marks. Cut only until the board bends easily, not all the way through.

5. Apply glue to the edges of the trough piece.

6. Fold the trough piece, cut side down (so that the bent side is on the inside of the trough), and align the corners to the corners of one of the end pieces.

7. Let it dry for a moment.

8. Turn it over and attach the other end piece.

9. Scrape out any glue that is on the inside of the trough; it should be smooth so that punching is accurate.

10. Glue the braces to the underside of the trough by abutting the edge of the brace to the trough and adhering it to the end pieces. This gives support while pressing down inside the trough.

11. Optional: Glue a piece of cord into the fold on the outside bottom of the trough. This gives something for the awl to go into and makes the trough last a bit longer.

12. Let it dry.

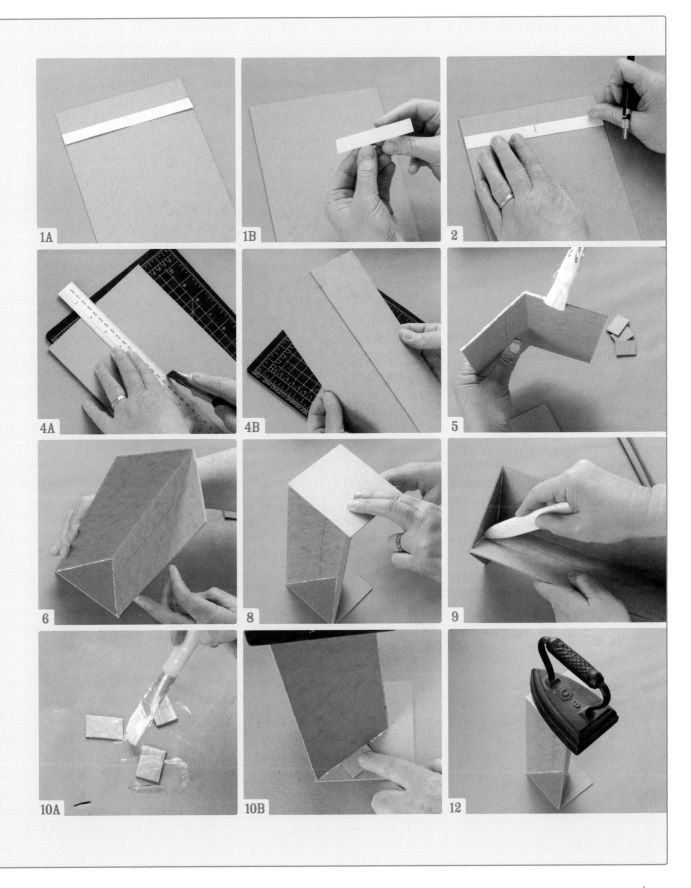

1A

1B

2

4A

4B

5

6

8

9

10A

10B

12

CHAPTER

2

Basic Techniques
and Definitions

Before you dive into a project, you'll need to understand the basic techniques you'll be working with, and the basic structure of a book. This chapter discusses the terms and techniques you should know.

Plan Your Project

Have a clear idea of how your finished book will look *before* you begin. Think through all the steps. This will help to ensure that you won't forget a crucial step. Know what tools and materials you will need. Consider how long the project will take and add a bit of extra time in case of mishaps.

If you develop a routine for performing your techniques, there will be less room for mistakes. For example, once you have established the grain of the paper, mark one of the corners with an arrow or line to indicate the direction of the grain, and always cut the length (grain direction) first.

Cut the project pieces that have to be the same size all at once, instead of at different times throughout your project. Perceptions of measurement can change: on the line, before the line, after the line—all are different and can alter the result of your work. You're more likely to be consistent if you cut your project pieces in groups based on size, rather than sporadically while you're working on your project.

Remember, the same adage applies in bookbinding as it does in woodworking: *Measure twice, cut once.*

The Framework of a Book

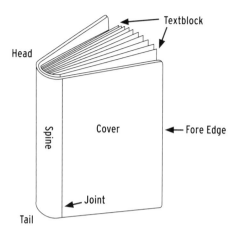

Head

Textblock

Spine

Cover

Fore Edge

Joint

Tail

Choose a Binding Style

A quarter binding is a design style for a book cover that is a combination of cover materials. It can be two colors of cloth or cloth and paper. The cloth width is one-quarter of the width of the book. Other styles include a full binding, where the book is covered in one piece of material, and a half binding, where there is a spine cover of one material and corner pieces of the same material; the center is another cloth or paper.

PLAN FOR TURN-INS

Turn-ins are the extra material or border around a board, usually book cloth or paper that is folded over and glued onto the inside of the board. Turn-ins ensure that the edges and corners of the boards are covered. The measurement for this extra material is about ½" (1.5 cm).

CHOOSE YOUR BOOK CLOTH

You can order many kinds of book cloth from bookbinding suppliers (see Resources on page 152). Two popular types are starch-filled cloth and paper-backed cloth. Starch-filled cloth can be thin or thick; the advantages of this type of cloth are that it is easier to manipulate than the paper-backed variety, and it's easy to wipe glue from its surface. Paper-backed cloth looks really nice, but it stains easily and can be very expensive.

If you want to use fabric from the fabric store instead of book cloth, we recommend that you use the heavy iron-on interfacing as a backing; otherwise, the glue will come through the weave and stain the right side of your cover material. Most fabrics you will find at a fabric store can be used for this. However, be careful of velvet, as it stains easily. Also, some upholstery fabrics are difficult to manipulate.

Determine the Grain

Grain direction is an overriding principle in bookbinding. Most of the materials used in bookbinding have a grain, and the grain of all parts should be laid in the same direction. Grain in paper is a result of how the fibers align when the paper is being manufactured. This alignment will affect how the paper will expand and contract. If pieces of a project are glued together such that the grains are conflicting, it is more likely that the project will warp. Here are a number of ways to determine the grain direction of materials. Throughout this book, the measurement with the grain will be underlined.

IN PAPER

Handmade paper is made by scooping paper slurry (bits of material suspended in water, with the consistency of oatmeal) with a tray on top of a screen. The screen is made of metal wires and allows the water

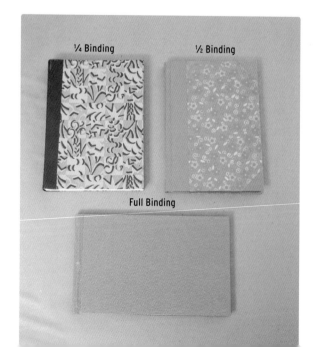

¼ Binding

½ Binding

Full Binding

How Much Paper is Needed?

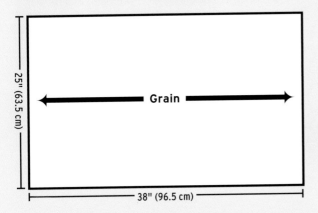

25" (63.5 cm)

38" (96.5 cm)

Grain

The projects in this book use a commercial sheet of text-weight paper where the grain runs long.

10.75" (27.5 cm)

7.25" (18 cm)

Always keep grain in mind when cutting paper. One sheet of commercial paper can be cut into ten pieces for a book with minimal waste (gray).

to drip through, leaving the material behind. A plain screen will only have a crisscross of wires (warp and weft, like fabric) called chain lines and laid lines. The chain lines are farther apart than the laid lines. Patterns can be woven into the screen. Often a watermark is woven into the screen to identify the papermaker. Makers of commercial paper as well as makers of handmade paper can use this type of mold to make paper. In moldmade papers where the chain lines and laid lines are visible, the grain runs with the chain lines. Hold the paper up to the light to see the lines.

In handmade paper, the fibers do not go in any particular direction so that the paper can be used to its best advantage.

In most other commercially made papers, you can feel the direction of the grain. Gently fold over the paper, but do not crease it. Carefully push the paper along the fold. The fold that has the least resistance shows the grain direction. If you cannot see or feel the grain, cut small tabs of paper in both directions and wet out the tabs. Look at how the paper curls. The tabs will curl in the direction of the grain.

Caution: Do not be fooled by the direction of any decoration on the paper. The decoration may have no relationship to the grain. Always check the direction of the grain using the aforementioned techniques.

ABOVE TOP Determine your paper's grain direction before you begin any project.

ABOVE BOTTOM The wetted tabs of a paper will curl in the direction of the grain.

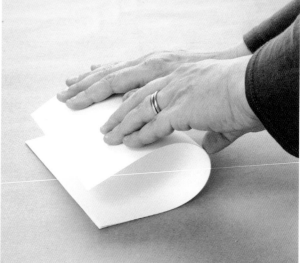

The grain goes in the direction of least resistance (right).

IN BOARD

To determine the grain in a board, gently try to bend the board. The grain direction follows the path that is easier to bend.

IN CLOTH

In cloth, the grain direction is the same as the selvedge (the edge of the cloth); it goes up the bolt of cloth.

USING GRAIN

The grain of all your materials should follow the direction of the book, head to tail. Even if the book has a landscape orientation, the grain of all your materials should follow the way the book will be held. As a method of working, try to always cut the length of each item first, and then cut the width.

How Much Paper Do You Need?

Having enough materials for a project is essential (see page 27). It is disappointing to run out of something midway through a project, or to discover that you need to order something and wait until it arrives before you can begin.

In the case of paper, sketch out the dimensions of the paper you are planning to use for the textblock. Mark the measurements of the sheet and the grain direction. Consider: What is the size of the final textblock? The textblock sections should be cut oversized first, then pressed, and then trimmed to the final size. Otherwise, the edges will be uneven. What are the dimensions of the oversized textblock? Draw those dimensions on the sketch of the paper. Into how many pieces can the paper be cut? How many are needed? Most paper is not strong enough to use only one piece of paper per section. Count on at least two pieces of paper per section. Then the paper is less likely to rip when sewn.

To help you to better understand this process, here is an example. The final dimensions of the textblock for the Friend-of-a-Friend Book covered in chapter 4 are 7" × 5" (18 × 13 cm). The rough cut of the height is approximately 7¼" (18 cm). The width cut is at least twice the final width plus a bit more. That is because the final width is measured with the pages folded in half. The rough cut of the width is approximately 10¾" (27.5 cm) with the page open, before folding. The paper used is 38" × 25" (96.5 × 63.5 cm) with the grain running lengthwise. The 7¼" (19 cm) dimension is cut along the 38" (96.5 cm) (long) dimension of the paper. From a 38" (96.5 cm) dimension, five strips measuring 7¼" (18 cm) can be cut. From the strips that are 7¼" × 25" (18 × 63.5 cm), two pieces that are 10¾" (27.5 cm) (plus extra) can be cut. That means ten individual 7¼" × 10¾" (19 × 27.5 cm) pieces of paper can be cut from this paper. Forty-eight individual pieces of paper are needed for this project; so five pieces of large paper are required.

Fold a Textblock

Start by cutting the paper oversized. Fold it in half to make sections, and then press it overnight, or for at least four hours. The paper will compress over time. If you do not press the paper before you make the book, the covers will no longer fit. Artificially compressing the pages ensures that the covers will always fit.

One sheet folded is called a folio. When more than one piece of paper is gathered together and folded to make the parts of a textblock, they can be called sections, gatherings, or quires.

MATERIALS

- Textblock paper
- Bone folder
- Press boards
- Weight

Instructions

1. Gather the individual pieces of paper that will comprise a section of the book.

2. Align these leaves, jogging them all together to the tail edge.

3. Hold the stack of paper at one lower corner.

4. Bring the opposite side of the paper over to this edge so that the edges are aligned.

5. Using the bone folder, make a crease along the fold from the bottom aligned edge upward or the center outward.

6. Stack the sections with the folded edges aligned.

7. Put the sections under press boards and a heavy weight. If the single stack is awkward, make two piles, each with the same number of sections. Press for a minimum of 4 hours or overnight.

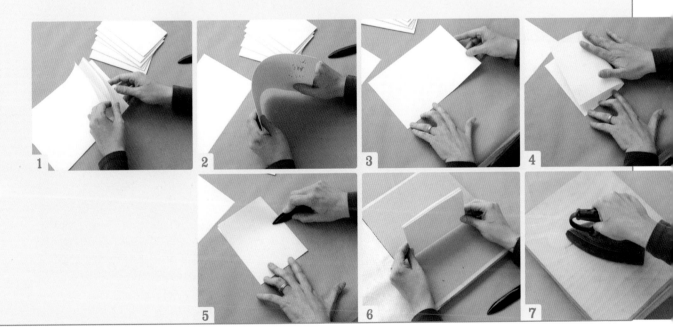

Fold a Single Large Textblock

For some books, one single section is used for the textblock instead of multiple sections. Folding and pressing a textblock of this size can be tough, and it is easy to lose too much of the width to trimming the paper if it's not done correctly.

MATERIALS

- Textblock paper
- Bone folder

Instructions

1. Gather the individual pieces of paper that will compose the textblock.

2. Align the leaves along the tail edge.

3. Fold them in half from both sides, aligning the papers along the fore edge.

4. Using the bone folder, press along the crease, from the center outward, in both directions.

Trim the Textblock

Bookbinding uses a lot of jigs and templates. Typically, you make them out of scrap materials, specifically for the project at hand. Although they are not intended to last forever, if you plan to make the same project over and over you can make the template out of a sturdy material and reuse it. Jigs and templates are simple tools that make it much easier to keep materials aligned and consistent. They also eliminate the need to remeasure. Here, create a jig to trim the textblock to its final size.

MATERIALS

- 1 piece of scrap binder's or mat board, cut to the dimensions of the textblock plus 1" (2.5 cm) in all directions
- 1 piece of scrap binder's or mat board, cut to the final dimensions of the textblock
- Strips of scrap binder's or mat board, cut to ¼" (6 mm) × the length of the large board
- Strips of scrap binder's or mat board, cut to ¼" (6 mm) the width of the large board minus ¼" (6 mm)
- Double-sided tape or glue
- Textblock sections
- Small weight
- Knife

Instructions

1. Stack longer strips of board until their height is equal to the thickness of the section + 1 board, and adhere them to the length of the large board with tape or glue.

2. Stack shorter strips of board until their height is equal to the thickness of the section + 1 board, and adhere them to the width of the large board. Make sure these strips, the walls of the jig, are square. The textblock should be able to fit securely within them.

3. Place a section of textblock into the jig with the folded edge along the length and the shorter edge along the width. Fit the final-sized board on top of it.

4. Holding the top board steady with a weight, make several slow cuts to the head of the section. The top board is a cutting guide so that all the pages are the same size. Cut the fore edge the same way.

5. Flip over and trim the tail end of the section, using the jig to align the pages and the top board as a guide.

6. Repeat until all the sections are trimmed to size.

Make a Template for Sewing

The type of template used most often in bookbinding is the one that enables the bookbinder to determine the sewing stations of a textblock. The project-specific templates in this book are included in the directions within the projects' directions.

MATERIALS

- 1 piece of waste paper or .010 pt. folder stock the same height as the sections
- Dividers
- Sewing tape
- Pencil
- Ruler
- Scissors
- Awl
- Punching trough

Instructions

1. Use a waste piece of paper or .010 pt. folder stock that is the same height as the sections to be sewn, and about 3" (7.5 cm)-wide. Fold the paper lengthwise.

2. Walk the dividers along the length of the paper. Divide the paper into one more than the number of sewing stations you need. So, if you want three sewing stations, divide the length of the paper into four equal parts. Shorten or lengthen the space between the legs of the divider to accomplish this. Trial and error and making small adjustments will make this task achievable, and it is easier, quicker, and more accurate than measuring. Three sewing stations are traditional and are used most often in this book. If a book is very large, more stations can be added for stability.

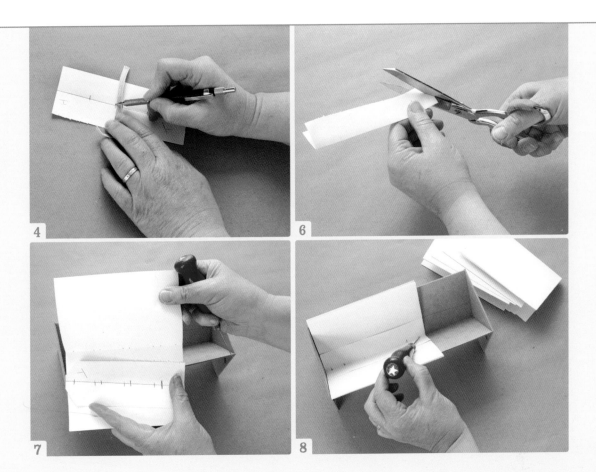

3. Press the legs into the paper to mark the three equal spaces.

4. Choose the sewing tape needed for the project (small book, thin tape; big book, wider tape). Starting at what will be the tail or bottom of the template, align one side of the sewing tape to the mark, with the fold mark on the right. Mark the width of the sewing tape. Leave enough room for the tape to lie flat when sewn. It should not be so tight that the tape is hindered, nor so loose that it will fall out. For three sewing stations there will be six marks along the template.

5. Measure and mark ½" (1 cm) away from each end of the template. Those marks are for the extra stitches called kettle stitches. There now should be eight marks on the template.

6. Miter the end of the template to help align it.

7. Put the section in the punching trough, open. Put the template inside the section; both the section and the template should be abutted to the end of the trough.

8. Using an awl, punch through the template and the section. Continue until all the sections are punched.

Sew the Textblock

Once you have a template ready, it's time to sew the textblock together.

MATERIALS

- Sections
- Sewing thread
- Needle
- Sewing tapes
- Masking tape
- Beeswax
- Press board

Gather your materials: the sections you want to sew, thread, needle, sewing tapes, masking tape, beeswax, and press boards.

Instructions

1. Thread a needle: Take a length of thread, about an arm's length. Pass the thread through the eye of the needle.

2. To catch the needle so that it does not detach from the thread, pierce the short end of the thread. It is easier to do this by flattening the thread a bit on a tabletop.

3. Bring the short end of the thread all the way down the shaft of the needle.

4. Pull the long end of the thread and slide the pierced part of the thread to the eye end of the needle.

5. Slide beeswax along the thread as desired. To detach the needle from the thread when you're finished sewing, cut the thread at the eye end.

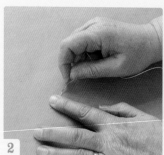

2

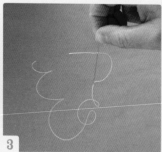

3

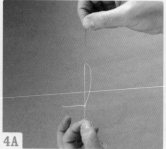

4A

4B

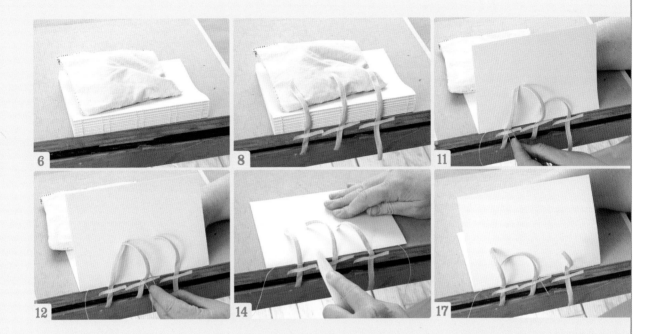

6. Place a press board along the edge of your table. The press board helps to keep the sections aligned while sewing. Place sections of the textblock to be sewn that have been punched at the edge of the press board.

7. Align the sewing tapes to the sewing stations punched in the section.

8. Tape the sewing tapes to the board with masking tape. Leave a length of the sewing tape below the section, as the tape should be longer than the thickness of all the sections as they form a textblock.

9. Open the section. Place a small weight inside.

10. Starting from the outside of the section, at the end hole, bring the threaded needle into the center of the section. Pull the thread, leaving about a 3" (7.5 cm) tail of thread.

11. Bring the thread to the next hole; sew from the inside to the outside of the section, around the tape, and back into the section at the next hole.

12. Continue the "in and out, around the tape" sequence until you reach the last hole of the section.

13. Pull the thread in the direction that you are sewing. This makes it less likely that you will rip the section. Keep the thread taut while you are sewing; it should not be lax in any way.

14. Take the weight out of the section. Close the section, and bone it down along the fold of the section. This helps the paper of the section absorb some of the bulk from the thread.

15. Place the next section on top of the section you just sewed.

16. Bring the thread up into the last hole of the new section, directly above the last hole the thread came out of in the section before.

17. Continue the in-out-around sewing of the previous section.

Sew the Textblock (continued)

18. At the end of the second section, tie a square knot with the tail that was left of the initial thread. Trim the tail of the thread to ½" (1.5 cm).

19. Add the third section as you did the second. Continue to sew as before.

20. At the end of the third section, sew a kettle stitch by bringing the needle between the current section and the one below it. This will form a loop of thread. Bring the needle through the loop of thread and pull straight up to catch the thread securely. This stitch will look like a / or \ along the end holes (depending on which direction the thread is wrapped; it doesn't matter, just be consistent). A kettle will be sewn at every loose end of a section.

21. Try not to pull so tightly that the ends of the textblock are pinched. Try to keep the thickness of the textblock even.

22. Continue until all the sections are sewn. At the end, sew two kettle stitches; you can tie them at the same place, or you can drop another section down for the second stitch.

 What to Do If You Run Out of Thread

If you run out of thread before your textblock is sewn, another piece of thread can be added onto the original piece. The technique to do so is called a weaver's knot. It is easiest to tie a weaver's knot on the inside of a section.

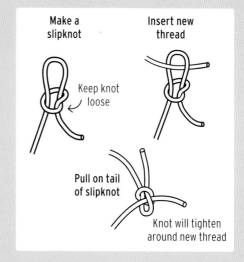

Make a slipknot

Keep knot loose

Insert new thread

Pull on tail of slipknot

Knot will tighten around new thread

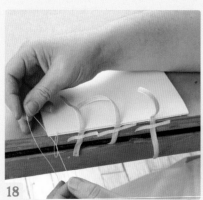
18

20

21

Cut the Materials

When cutting materials, you should hold your ruler, straightedge, or triangle firmly and make as many light cuts with the knife as necessary. Keep the blades sharp. Try to keep the knife parallel to the object.

Glue the Materials

As a general rule, glue out (i.e., apply glue) the thinner of the two materials. Thin material will have a stronger reaction to the moisture in the glue or paste, and will expand and curl. Let the material relax before you try to adhere it to something else. Allowing the thinner materials to react to the moisture in the adhesive reduces the incidence of wrinkling. It is fine if that means reapplying the adhesive. Use the largest brush you can in relation to the object being glued. Make sure there is a piece of waste paper under anything that will be glued. Glue out large pieces with a star pattern: Spread the glue from the center outward, holding the piece with your fingertips. Glue straight off the pieces. Do not back up with the glue brush, or glue could get onto the wrong side of the piece and stain it.

DRYING TIME

Drying entails placing a board on top of the item to be dried, and weighting it down with a weight to ensure that the item remains flat. Check the item periodically; if it is cold to the touch, it is not yet completely dry.

MAKING PASTE

You can make paste in the microwave. In a small bowl, mix 1 tablespoon (15 ml) of wheat starch paste with 5 tablespoons (75 ml) of distilled water. Let it sit for 15 minutes, and then stir. Microwave the mixture for 30 seconds. Stir again and look at the consistency. It should be smooth and not too watery. You can recook for 10 seconds if necessary. The paste will keep in the refrigerator for a while, usually at least 1 week. Water can be added to the paste to thin it out if needed.

Instant paste is nice because you can make only the amount you need. Spoon the powder into distilled water and stir until smooth. Add as much water as you need to reach the desired consistency.

Other Techniques

Here are a few additional techniques that will come in handy as you explore the projects in this book.

BONING DOWN

Boning down means rubbing down a fold or any material with your bone folder to make a neat, tight crease or to make sure something has adhered well, with no air bubbles. When working with a delicate material, you can use the bone folder over waste paper.

SCORING

Scoring means creating a crease with the tip of the bone folder. The thickness of the bone folder may impact the crease. If this happens, crease slightly *before* a mark line rather than directly on it. The amount of space that the crease takes up can change the measurement.

MITERING

Mitering is an angled cut. This is used often to cut away unnecessary material, especially when covering the corners of a book cover. Removing a triangular piece of material at the corner removes the extra that can interfere and also makes sure the corner is covered.

TIP | **Tying a Square Knot**

A square knot is a very secure knot used during the sewing of a textblock. To tie a square knot, remember "right over left, left over right" when moving to join the threads together.

Glue the Cover

Use your gluing skills to attach the cover paper to the board.

MATERIALS

- Glue
- Glue brush
- Waste sheet or scrap paper
- Scissors
- Bone folder

Instructions

1. Place the cover paper to be glued, nice side down, on a piece of waste paper.

2. Hold the brush in your fist, and dip it into the glue. Stroke the paper in a star pattern from the center out, applying an even coat of glue.

3. With your other hand, make sure the paper to be glued does not move around and get glue on the front of it. The nice side of the paper might react to the moisture in the adhesive. Be ready to keep the paper flat with the brush and your other hand.

4. Place the glued-out cover paper onto binder's board.

5. Bone down the paper so that it adheres firmly and there are no air bubbles.

2A

2B

5

6A

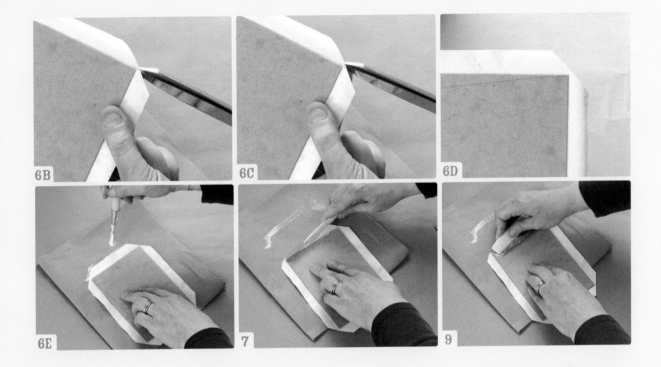

6. Take the points off the corners or miter the corners. The miter should be about two board thicknesses away from the point of the corner. Cut a small square of material away from the paper at the point of the corner. This takes away extra bulky material. It is okay to reapply glue to the turn-ins if they have dried out.

7. Fold the extra material (the turn-ins) over onto the opposite face (back side) of the board. Turn the head and tail turn-ins over first, then do the turn-ins on the fore edge. Make sure the paper is very tight and smooth along the edge of the board.

8. Use the tip of the bone folder to make sure the material at the corners is tight where it will bend along the edge.

9. Turn in the fore edge and spine edges of the paper. Again, use the bone folder to make sure the paper is tight along the edges.

> **TIP** **Don't Forget to Glue**
>
> Make sure to glue the turn-in tight to the board on the edges.

Studio
Projects

Albums

Albums are a great way to enhance flat objects, and a great way to keep them protected and organized. Each leaf or page is a piece of artwork unto itself. So, while you're planning out your album, think about each page individually in addition to considering the entire album as a cohesive unit. Look at the placement of objects, the grouping of objects, and the story each page tells and its place in the flow of the whole.

This chapter will introduce you to three styles of album: the Woven Album, the Stub Album, and the Accordion Album with Frames. Start with the Woven Album to get a feel for its flexibility in terms of the type of paper you can use. Turn it into a notebook with paper you enjoy writing on. Turn it into a sketchbook or watercolor journal with heavy drawing paper or watercolor paper. Or turn it into a photo album—the weaving will accommodate thick photo paper easily. The Stub Album also makes a great photo album. It features built-in compensation, which is great for photos or other two-dimensional items you want to let people browse through. Finally, the Accordion Album with Frames is a portable gallery. It can show off flat work as well as three-dimensional items, all in built-in frames. Also, you can fold it up for easy storage.

A nipping press ensures that the paper is pressed and that the glue adheres properly.

Here are some points to consider when beginning an album and choosing the best structure for your project:

- How many items (such as photos, drawings, or three-dimensional objects) will the album hold? Will the items be on both sides of the leaves or just one? Make sure the structure you choose will accommodate them.

- How heavy are your items? If they are heavy enough, you may need a heavier-weight text paper to support them. This could range from watercolor paper to mat board to a heavy-weight drawing paper. The pages should support your objects. However, heavier-weight text papers mean stiffer pages. Stiffer pages in the book won't turn as well, and could lead to their own structural issues, such as cracking. Make sure you find the right balance of support and usability.

- Will your items be displayed both horizontally and vertically? If so, you will need a larger page to accommodate this. If you're planning to use a landscape format, consider the weight of the paper and how it will be supported on the fore edge. An item that is too heavy for the supporting paper will cause the supporting paper to rip, sag, and not display or shelve correctly. Choose a support that is sturdier—as thick or heavy, or thicker or heavier—than the item.

- How will your items be attached to the page? You could use solutions such as slots at the item corners, photo-mounting corners, or mounting strips—or you could make an album with frames.

- What color pages will bring out the best in the items on them? Black is great. It has a traditional look and makes colors pop, but it scratches easily. White is classic, but it can look dirty easily.

- Does the album need a title label on the cover? Paper labels are easy to make with word processing applications. Experiment with text boxes and borders.

- How about embellishments? Where could you easily integrate a ribbon, beads, or other collage material? You need to consider the collective height of any inclusions when planning your album and how it will function. Adding enough room for the inclusions at the spine when making the book will help the album function well into the future.

The items you use in your album don't have to be two-dimensional, but if so, make sure you choose a structure and paper that will support them.

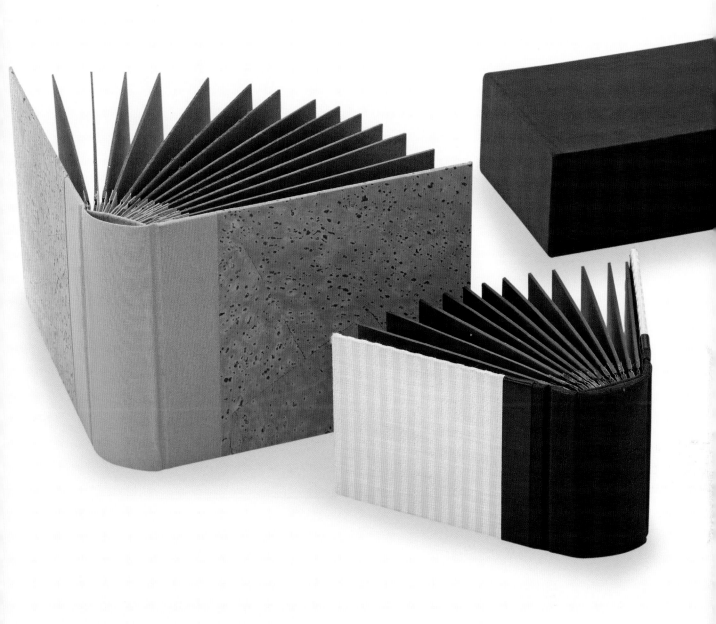

Think about what color pages will
bring out the best in the items on
them, and find the perfect cover to
complement them.

STUDIO PROJECT

Woven Album

This book looks like it is put together with mysterious weaving. Here the secret is revealed: It is a modified Jacob's ladder. It opens flat and can accommodate any number of leaves. The weaving is the compensation for the added items so that the book remains flat when filled.

This structure is a great way to collect individual pages. It opens completely flat, and the weaving provides compensation for any added inclusions. It is important to be patient with the weaving in order to create a sturdy, stable binding.

SIZE

6" × 8" (15 × 20 cm), landscape orientation

TIME

Time: approx. 3½ hours
Prep: 1 hour
Make: 2 hours
Downtime/Drying time:
30 minutes

TOOLS

- Bone folder
- Knife
- Ruler
- Glue brush
- Pencil
- Dividers

OPTIONAL TOOLS

- Microspatula
- Weight

MATERIALS

- Heavyweight paper, with a final cut of 6" × 8" (15 × 20 cm); an even number of leaves works best
- Two 6" × 8" (15 × 20 cm) sheets of .010 pt. *or* .020 pt. board
- Two 6" × 8" (15 × 20 cm) pieces of .067 pt. cover board
- Enough Moriki, *or* another strong Japanese paper, *or* any other paper that is strong and flexible, to create six 20" × ½" (50 × 1.5 cm) laces, double thickness
- Four 7" × 9" (17.5 × 23 cm) pieces of decorative paper
- One 6" × ½" (15 × 1.5 cm) piece of .010 pt. board
- 3 pieces of scrap board for the jig: 1 piece longer than the length of the page and at least one-quarter of the width of the page, for a base; and 2 pieces for walls, one the length of the page and at least ½" (1.5 cm) wide, and one the length of the width of the base piece and at least ½" (1.5 cm) wide
- Double-sided tape
- PVA
- Waste paper

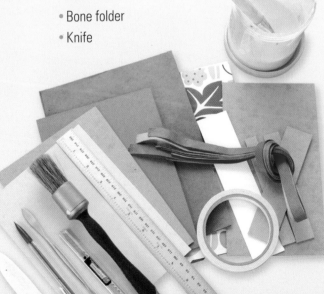

The tools and materials required include a bone folder, pencil, knife, glue brush, ruler, dividers, heavyweight paper, binder's board, decorative paper, and glue.

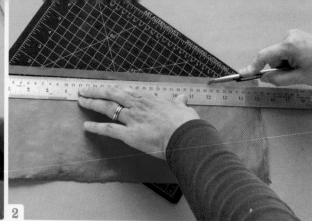

INSTRUCTIONS

Make Moriki Laces

1. Glue out one length of Moriki paper and fold it in half lengthwise, ending up with a <u>24</u>" × 3" (<u>61</u> × 7.5 cm) piece, creating a long strip of double-sided paper. Allow this to dry.

2. Once the Moriki paper is dry, measure and cut 6 lengths to 24" × ½" (61 × 1.5 cm). Allow for approximately ½" (1.5 cm) of each strip for each sheet of leaf/page. The total width of all the laces should not be more than half the width of the text-block. If you are making a smaller album, reduce the number of laces.

Make the Cover Boards

The cover boards are made of two boards (one .010 pt. board and one binder's board), each covered on one side with decorative paper. These two boards are then sandwiched together with the laces secured between them.

3. On waste paper, glue out the decorative paper and cover one side of each of the .010 pt. boards. Bone them down, miter the corners, and adhere the turn-ins. Set them aside under a weight to dry. Repeat with the cover boards. Caution: The .010 pt. board will react to the moisture in the glue. It is important to keep them under a weight until they are dry, to keep them flat.

4. Cover the binder's board covers with decorative paper.

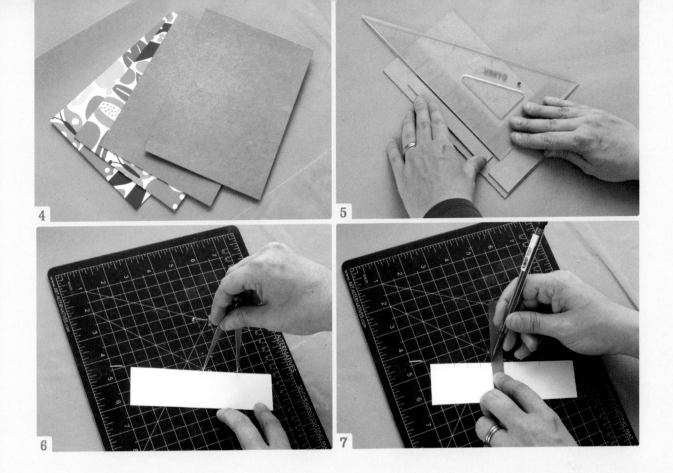

Make a Template for Cutting the Slots

This will hold the leaves/pages in place while you are cutting the slots for weaving. The base should be large enough to hold each leaf/page steady and provide a cutting surface. The sides will brace the leaf/page and the template so that the cuts are positioned correctly and are aligned.

5. Position the shorter wall piece along the bottom of the base and secure it with double-sided tape. Position the longer wall piece along the edge of the base and abutting the shorter wall piece. Make sure they are square to each other. Secure with double-sided tape.

6. Cut 1 piece of .010 pt. board to 6" × ½" (15 × 1.5 cm), the height of the leaves x one-quarter of the width. Using dividers, divide the length of the .010 pt. board into 4 equal measurements. Mark the 3 spots along the interior of the .010 pt. board.

7. This is the middle of 3 marks. On either side of this mark, measure and mark 1 line that is the width of the Moriki laces (½" [1.5 cm]).

8. Mark the spaces, alternating between "A" and "B" as the marking for each space.

> ### TIP
>
> Thick paper is a good choice for your heavy-weight paper because it will support the weaving as well as the objects attached to the leaves.

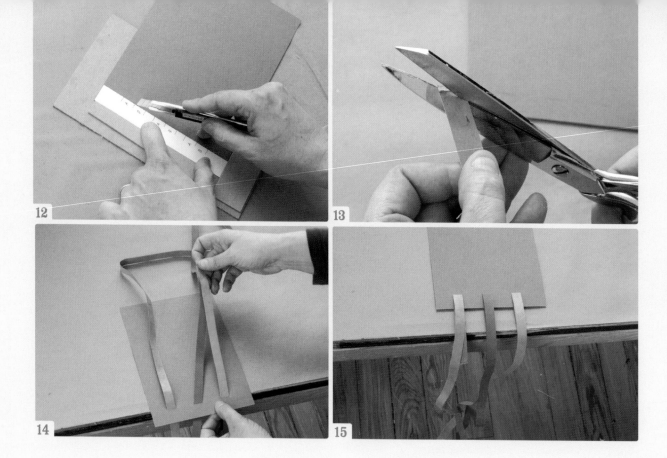

Cut the Slots into the Paper

9. Make 2 equal piles of the interior leaves/pages. One will have the "A" cuts and one will have the "B" cuts.

10. Abut an interior paper to the scrap board on the jig, aligning the spine edge and tail within the walls. Align the template along the spine edge and on top of the page, and abutting the walls of the jig.

11. Cut 3 slots designated "A" on the page. Continue with all the "A" pages (see Tip, page 51).

12. Change to the "B" pile and cut 3 slots designated "B" on all pages in the other pile (see Tip, page 51).

Weave the Book

13. Begin with a sheet of paper marked "A." Set the work on the edge of your table, spine out. Miter the ends of the Moriki laces. Pointed ends are easier to weave.

14. Working from underneath to the top, lace separate strips through each of the 3 slots, leaving a 3" to 4" (7.5 to 10 cm) tail on the bottom. A thin bone folder or microspatula is helpful here.

15. Fold the strips down *cleanly* toward the spine. Bone them down.

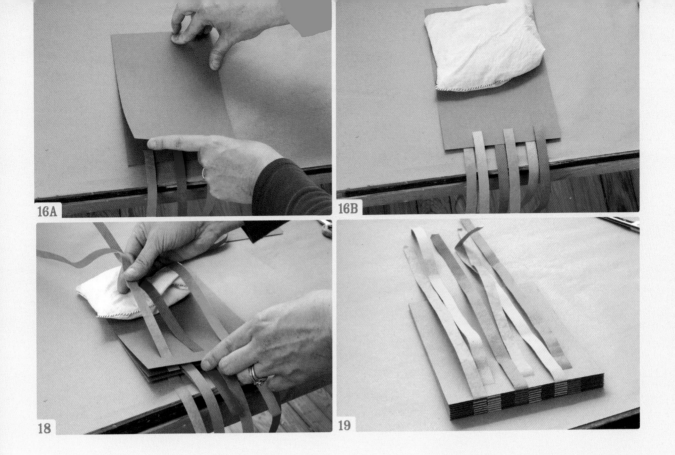

16A

16B

18

19

16. Place a sheet of paper marked "B" on top of the paper marked "A," squaring up at all the edges, and repeat the lacing procedure with 3 other strips. A weight will be helpful here.

17. Alternate the "A" sheets and "B" sheets. The laces will wrap around the spine edge of the pages. Place an "A" sheet on top and lace the "A" strips through. Do not pull too tightly or the "B" page will bend and crease. Square up nicely and gently, and cleanly fold the strip around the "B" page underneath to square up and set tension.

18. Tails of the "B" laces will fold under the "A" pages so that all the extra lengths of the lacing strips are side by side and touching the table. Fold the "B" strip toward the spine. Make sure the fold of the laces is flush to the spine as each leaf/page is added.

19. Continue in this manner until the textblock is done. Set aside.

TIP **Positioning of Slots A + B**

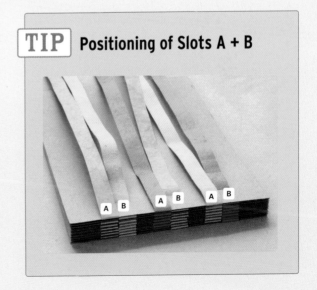

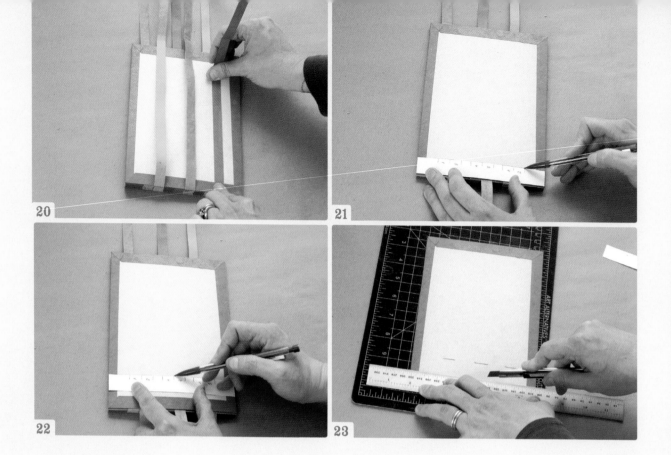

Mark the Covered .010 pt. Boards for the Slots

20. Align the .010 pt. boards to the textblock with the covered side facing the textblock. Look at the laces. One set of laces will be on top of the leaf/page. This set will require 2 slots to weave the laces so that they end up on top of the cover board. The other set will only require 1 slot as it is in the correct position to lace.

21. Once the boards are aligned, align the template along the spine edge of the cover. Mark 1 line that includes both slots ("A" and "B") at each station.

22. Reposition the template to align the long edge of the template to the line you just made for the double slots. This will indent the second slot by the width of the template. Mark *only* the lace position that requires the second slot to end up on top of the cover board.

23. Cut those slots.

24. Lace the .010 pt. boards in, alternating the "A" and "B" laces. Trim the laces to an even length, about 1½" (4 cm).

25. Glue out the laces, adhere them to the board, and bone them down.

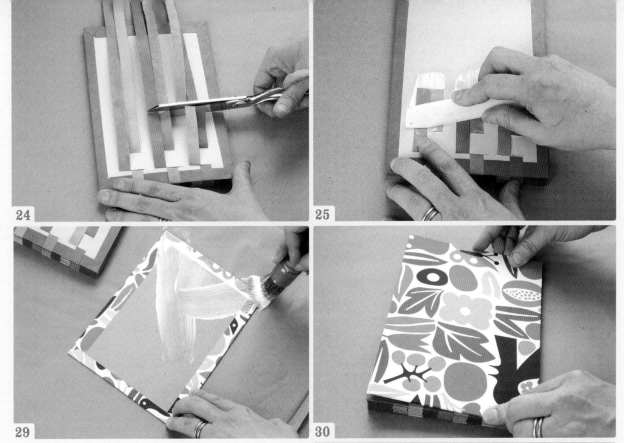

26. Turn the textblock over and mark and cut slots in the same way for the second .010 pt. board.

27. Lace the .010 pt. boards in, alternating the "A" and "B" laces.

28. Trim the laces to an even length, about 1½" (4 cm). Glue out the laces, adhere them to the board, and bone them down.

29. On a piece of waste paper, glue out the binder's board covers.

30. Align and adhere binder's board to the .010 pt. covers.

31. Bone down and repeat on the other side.

32. Leave under a weight until they are dry.

Stiff-Leaved Stub Album

STUDIO PROJECT

Stubs allow an album to accommodate items of varying thickness easily. They also let you include a flexible hinge on the carrier sheet; the stubs lift the leaf out of the hinge and allow it to lay flat. For books holding larger, heavier items, you can make the stubs thicker. Stubbed bindings are a great way to display a few items in a formal manner while presenting them together as a collection.

SIZE

Any size; the model we used is 5" × 6" (12.5 × 15 cm), landscape

TIME

Time: approx. 3½ hours

Prep: 1 hour

Make: 2 hours

Downtime/Drying time: approx. 30 minutes

TOOLS

- Bone folder
- Glue brush
- Ruler
- Weight

OPTIONAL TOOLS

- 90-degree triangle

MATERIALS

- 32 pieces of 4-ply museum board: 16 pieces for the pages and 16 pieces for the stubs. In this model, we used 4¾" × 5½" (12 × 14 cm) pieces for the pages and 4¾" × ¼" (12 cm × 6 mm) pieces for the stubs.

- 1 more book cloth hinge than the number of pages. In this model, we used seventeen 4¾" × 2" (12 × 5 cm) pieces.

- Cloth for cover: height larger than the cover boards by 2 × the turn-ins; width enough to cover one-quarter of the width of the boards, plus the spine thickness (5½" × 6" [14 × 15 cm])

- 1 piece of .020 pt. or light card stock, cut to 5" (12.5 cm) × the width of the textblock.

- 2 pieces of binder's board covers cut to slightly larger than the textblock × the width of the textblock. In this model, we used 5" × 6" (12.5 × 15 cm) pieces.

- Light paper, cut to the height of the covers × the width of the textblock. In this model, we used 5" × 6" (12.5 × 15 cm) pieces.

- 1 spine piece of .020 pt. board or light card stock, cut to the height of the covers x the width of the textblock

- Decorative paper

- Hemp cord or cotton butcher's twine

- PVA

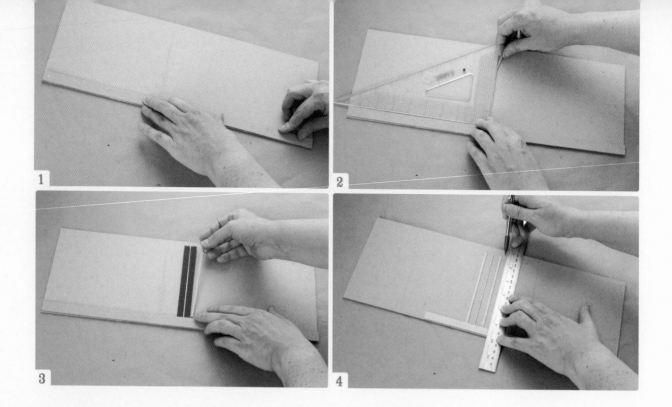

MATERIALS FOR THE JIG

- 1 piece of scrap board large enough to accommodate two stubs and two pages with a slight space in between them. In this model, we used a piece measuring 13¾" × 6" (35 × 15 cm).

- 1 piece of scrap board up to which align the stubs and pages. In this model, we used a piece measuring ½" × 13¾" (1.5 × 35 cm).

- 3 pieces of .020 pt. or light card stock to use as spacers between the stubs and pages:

- 1 piece that is 1 thickness of stub/page material + 2 cloth thicknesses × the height of the page; in this model, we used a piece measuring ¹⁄₁₆" × 4¾" (2 mm × 12 cm)

- 2 pieces that are 4 × the thickness of the page/stub material + 4 cloth thicknesses × the height of the page; in this model, we used pieces measuring ⅛" × 4¾" (3 mm × 12 cm)

INSTRUCTIONS

Make the Jig

1. Mark the center of the large piece of scrap board. Mark the center of the long strip of scrap board. Adhere the strip of scrap board along the long edge of the large piece of scrap board so that the centers line up.

2. Align the triangle along the long strip at the center point. Adhere the very small (¹⁄₁₆" [2 mm]) spacer vertically next to the triangle.

3. Place a stub on either side of the small spacer. On the other side of both stubs, align and adhere the larger spacers vertically. Try not to have the spacer very tight against the stub, as it will be difficult to remove it later.

4. Draw a line ¼" (6 mm) away from the left and right vertical edges of the large spacers. Extend this line to the long strip of scrap board so that it will be visible when you apply the cloth hinge. You will use this line to help align the cloth hinges.

Make the Textblock

Each leaf is made of a stub and a page, which is hinged to another stub and page.

5. Place a stub-page pair in the jig to the right and left of the small spacer. Make sure each piece is aligned along the bottom as they sit on the long strip of scrap board.

6. Glue a cloth hinge and align it to the marks on the bottom of the jig. The cloth should be the height of the pieces and should extend over the stubs and onto part of the pages.

7. Bone down the cloth.

8. Carefully remove the leaf and stub from the jig and set them aside to let them dry.

9. Repeat steps 5 through 8 for the remaining pages and stubs.

10. Fold all of the completed pages in half, with the cloth hinge on the inside. Be sure to align the edges so that all of them are even.

11. Each two-page section will now be adhered to another two-page section in the same manner as above to form four-page sections. Put the folded two-page sections into the jig. Glue up the cloth hinge and adhere. Bone them down.

12. Continue until all of the two-page sections are formed into four-page sections.

13

14

15A

15B

16A

16B

Make the Textblock (continued)

13. Adhere the four-page sections in the same way to make eight-page sections. Continue until all the sections are adhered into a single textblock, with the stubs at the spine edge. Place them under a weight to let them dry.

14. The two remaining hinges will attach the textblock to the case. One half of the hinge will be adhered to the textblock, and the other half will remain unglued until the case is attached. Fold a cloth hinge lengthwise and glue out one side. Adhere it to the textblock with the fold at the spine edge. Repeat on the other side.

15. The spine of the textblock will naturally take on a round shape. Encourage it to be symmetrical by gently pushing the fore edge. The round spine edge should be one-third of a circle, which is very slightly rounded (not as round as half a circle). Make sure the head and tail of the pages are aligned. Place the textblock under a weight and apply a light layer of PVA to the spine. Let it dry.

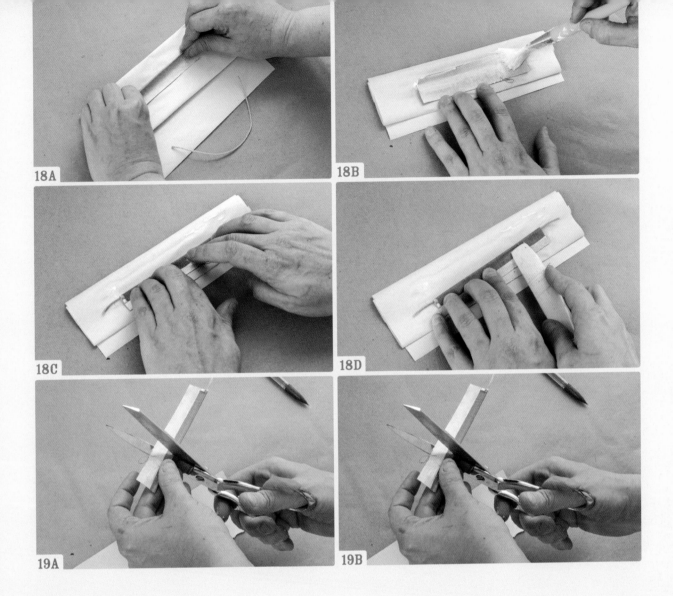

18A 18B

18C 18D

19A 19B

Make Headbands (optional)

Headbands are decorative elements that sit on top of the head and tail of a textblock. You can buy headbands, or you can easily make them out of a piece of cord or twine and some book cloth.

16. Wrap a piece of waste paper along the spine of your textblock. Mark the edges of the spine on the waste paper and remove it. The marks give the width of the spine.

17. Cut a length of book cloth 1" (2.5 cm) x twice the thickness of the textblock, and cut a piece of cord the length of the cloth.

18. Crease the width of the cloth about ¼" (6 mm) down from the top. Glue out up to the crease and a bit over it. Place the cord along the crease. Fold the cloth over and bone along the edge of the cord to make sure the cloth is tight around it.

19. Cut a piece of headband to the width of the spine. Glue it up below the cord and place this onto the spine of the book, with the wrapped cord sitting along the head and tail, being sure to bone it down.

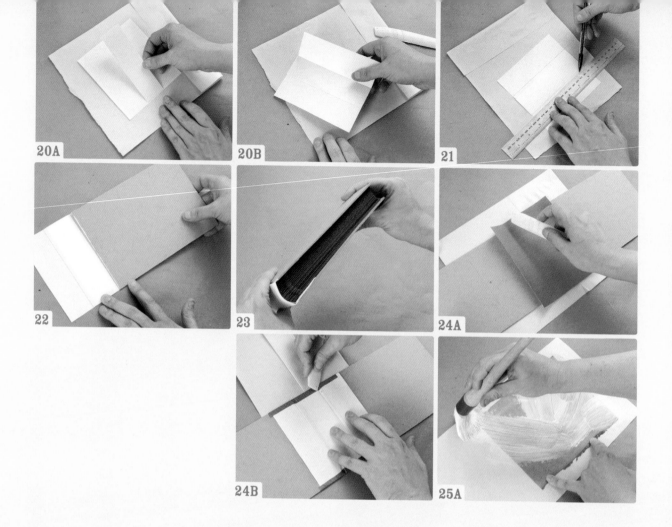

Make the Case

20. Adhere the spine piece to the center of the light paper. Fold the paper along the edge of the .020 pt. board to give it a clean edge.

21. On the reverse side of this piece, mark a line ¼" (5 mm) out from the spine piece on both sides.

22. Apply a line of glue the width of the glue brush along the spine edge of a cover piece. Align it to the marks on the side of the spine piece. Glue it down. Adhere the other cover.

23. Wrap the cover around the textblock, keeping the round portion of the textblock even. Set it under a weight and let it dry.

Cover the Case

24. Remove the case. Place it on a piece of waste paper with the .020 pt. board facing down. Glue up the 5½" × 6" (14 × 15 cm) cloth and gingerly place it over the spine. Bone it down, working it into the grooves of the front boards. Flip it over and work down the turn-ins, working out any wrinkles at the joints. Place it on a textblock to dry, working a curve into the spine strip again.

25. Working on the case only, remove the textblock. Glue up the decorative paper and adhere it to the front and back cover boards, going over the cloth about ⁄16" (2 mm). Bone it down. Flip the boards to miter the corners and work the turn-ins. Repeat for the other side.

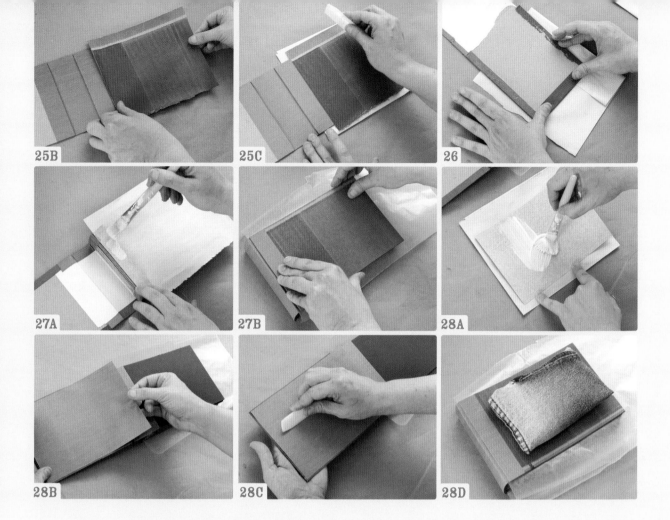

Case In the Textblock

26. With the textblock in the case, place a piece of waste paper under the cloth hinge of the textblock. Carefully open the case, being sure to not shift anything.

27. Glue up the hinge, remove the waste paper, and close the case onto the glued hinge. Pound it down. Flip the book and repeat this step on the other side. Set it under a weight to dry.

28. Open the covers, and glue up a piece of 5½" × 6" (14 × 15 cm) book cloth. Carefully align this on the inner cover board, covering a portion of the hinge. Bone it down. Repeat for the other side. Place it under a weight to dry.

Accordion Album with Frames

Accordion books are very flexible and can be adapted for many projects. Framing gives special emphasis to artwork. Why not combine the two? This book provides one solution to displaying, housing, and protecting two-dimensional art, all at the same time.

Note: The back mat board is called the mount board. The front is called the frame.

SIZE

Any size; the model we used has 6 panels and is 6½" × 7½" (16.5 × 19 cm)

TIME

Time: approx. 2 hours
Prep: 1 hour
Make: 1 hour
Downtime/Drying time: approx. 10 minutes

The materials required include wheat paste, 4-ply mat board, Japanese paper, photos to be framed, book cloth hinges, and glue brushes.

TOOLS

- Mat knife
- Bone folder
- Ruler
- Pencil
- Small glue brush
- Small paste brush
- Weights
- Scissors
- Self-healing mat or scrap board to cut on

OPTIONAL TOOLS

- Mat cutter
- Squeeze bottle with glue
- Hinging tape

MATERIALS

- Photos or other flat items to be framed. In this model, we used six 4" × 6" (10 × 15 cm) landscape-orientation photos.

- 4-ply (.040 pt.) mat board in any color. The height and width are determined by the size of the items to be framed, plus the border around them. In this model, we used twelve 6" × 7½" (15 × 19 cm) pieces.

- One strip of Japanese paper (kozo or mulberry) for each panel, ½" (1.5 cm) wide x slightly less than the width of the panel tall. For the model, we used 6 pieces measuring 7" × ½" (17.5 × 1.5 cm).

- Two ¼" × ½" (6 mm × 1.5 cm) Japanese paper (kozo or mulberry) hinges for each item, to attach objects to the mount board.

- Strips of book cloth, one fewer than the total number of panels. The height should be 2 × the height of the mount board + a bit extra. The width should be the amount of gap space between the panels + the amount needed to attach either side to the mount board—approximately ½" (1.5 cm) total. For the model, we used five 13" × 2" (33 × 5 cm) pieces cut from one 13" × 3¾" (33 × 9.5 cm) piece.

- PVA

- Wheat paste

- Waste paper

INSTRUCTIONS

Measure and Mark for the Photos

The lower part of the artwork usually has the highest concentration of color and image, which to the eye makes the image sink down. So when you're framing, widen the bottom border of the frame to push the image up and balance the effect of the frame around the art. This is referred to as visual center.

1. Decide how much of a border will be around each item. The standard is to make the top and sides the same size and the bottom slightly larger. This will give it visual center. Also determine the amount that the frame will overlap the item. This will be minimal, about ⅛" to ¼" (3 to 6 mm). For the model, we used 1¼" (3 cm) for the bottom border and 1" (2.5 cm) for the other three sides.

2. Cut the mat boards all to the same size, 2 pieces for each panel. For the model, we cut 12 pieces of mat board (4-ply, .040 pt.) to 6" × 7½" (15 × 19 cm) with the grain running vertically.

3. On half of the pieces of mat board, draw cut lines with a pencil and a ruler. These will become the frames. For the model, we marked 1" (2.5 cm) on three sides and 1¼" (3 cm) on one side (the bottom).

Cut the Frames

4. Hold the ruler firmly and make several cuts with the knife until the mat board is cut clean through. Be very careful at the corners. The cuts should be sharp; check the cutting edge on your knife frequently to ensure that you have a sharp blade.

TIP | How Much of a Border?

When determining the dimensions of the border, use a piece of waste paper to see what the border will look like before cutting anything.

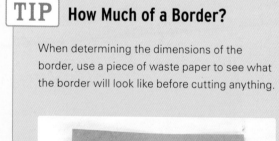

Attach the Frames to the Mount Boards

5. Align 1 frame (face down) and 1 mount board along their top edges.

6. Paste out a strip of Japanese paper on a piece of waste paper.

7. Cover the seam where the mats meet with the Japanese paper strip.

8. Rub down the paper strip gently with a bone folder.

9. Leave it in place until the strips are dry so that they do not stick together. Repeat until all the frames are attached to the mount boards.

Measure and Mark the Mats

10. With a pencil (or dividers), mark the mount boards ¼" (5 mm) away from the side edges. The cloth hinges will be attached to the mount boards ¼" (5 mm) from the edge, with a ¼" (5 mm) gap between each one.

Hint: The space between the mats is the thickness of the two panels, plus the thickness of the book cloth hinge. This will ensure that there is enough room for the accordion to fold flat. If you are using 2-ply board, or items on both sides (a double mat), measure the thickness of the materials to calculate the gap in between each one.

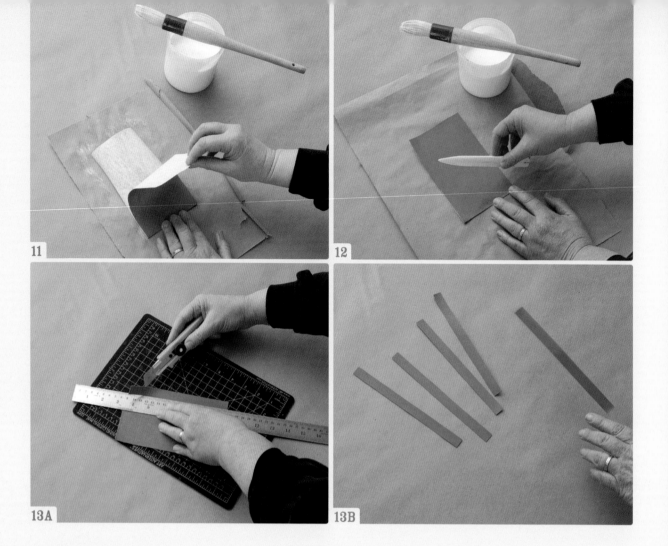

Make the Cloth Hinges

11. Glue the book cloth and fold it in half onto itself, being sure to align the edges.

12. Rub it down with the bone folder, being careful not to let excess glue get on the book cloth. Let it dry.

13. Measure, mark, and cut 5 pieces measuring ¾" × 6½" (2 × 16.5 cm).

TIP

Try putting items on both sides of your pages! If you try this, add extra panels on each end to make covers that protect the items on the outside.

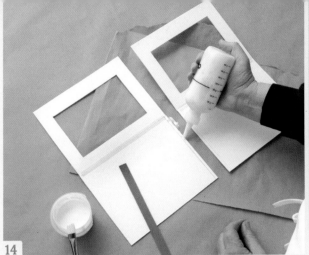

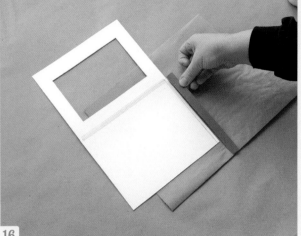

Attach the Hinges to the Mats

14. Set 1 mount board on a piece of waste paper and lightly glue out the ¼" (5 mm) mark on the edge of the mat board. **Hint:** A squeeze bottle with glue is helpful here.

15. Place the folded end of the cloth hinge at the top of the mount board.

16. Align one side of the cloth hinge to the ¼" (5 mm) mark.

17. Rub down the cloth hinge with the bone folder.

18. Lightly glue the next mount board at the ¼" (5 mm) mark. **Hint:** Abut a ruler to the bottom edge of the mount boards that are being joined so that they are aligned.

19. Align the other side of the cloth hinge to the ¼" (5 mm) mark, leaving a ¼" (5 mm) gap between the mount boards.

20. Rub down the cloth hinge.

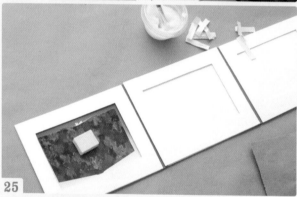

Attach the Items

The items are attached with Japanese paper and paste, because this way they can be removed without damaging them. The paper can be cut away from the mount board, and the paste is water-soluble for clean removal.

23. Measuring from the bottom of the mount board, mark where the bottom edge of the photo should be.

24. Measuring from the side of the mount board, mark where the side edge of the photo should be.

25. Place the item within those marks and put a small weight on the item. Close the frame and check to make sure it looks correctly aligned. Adjust as necessary.

26. On a piece of waste paper, paste out a small piece of Japanese paper.

Attach the Hinges to the Mats (continued)

21. Put a small weight on the cloth hinge and let it dry for a few minutes. Continue with the rest of the hinges and mount boards until all are joined.

22. When dry, trim the end of the cloth hinge to the bottom edge of the mount board so that the hinge runs the full length of the mount board. **Hint:** This is easiest to do with the inside of the mats flush to the work surface. The edge of the mat will serve as a guide for where to cut.

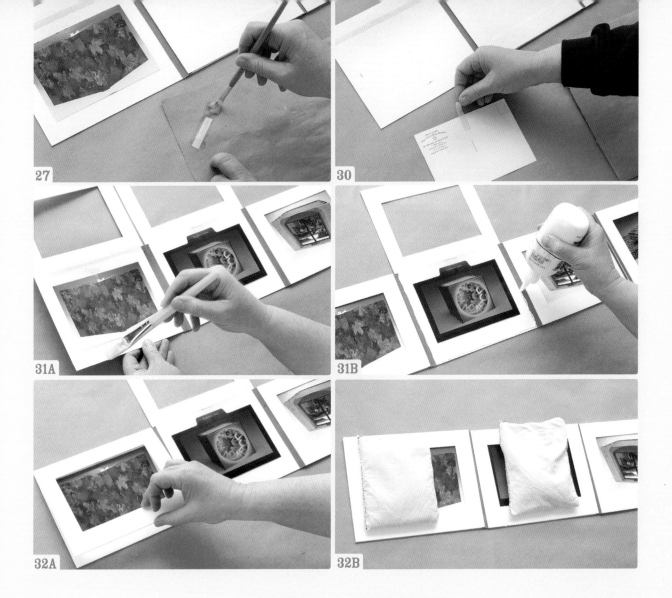

27. Adhere about half of the Japanese paper to the center of the top edge of the item vertically, paste side up. Half of the paper hinge should be sticking out from under the item.

28. Align the item at the marks on the mount board.

29. Paste out another small piece of Japanese paper.

30. Place the second piece of Japanese paper horizontally, paste side down, across the first piece of Japanese paper to form a "T hinge." The second piece of Japanese paper will hold the paper that is attached to the item in place.

Seal the Mats

31. Apply a thin line of glue to the perimeter of the mount board. Be careful not to get glue on the middle of the cloth hinge where it will be visible. A squeeze bottle is helpful.

32. Close the mat and put a weight on it until it is dry. Continue with the remaining mats until all the mats are sealed.

This album can be stored closed up or displayed open. Try adding a ribbon or tie for closure prior to sealing the first and last mats.

Books

Why make your own books? It's another form of self-expression that is not always considered. From the content, to the structure, to the materials, to the color combinations, to the decorations, every aspect speaks about the person who made it. For those daunted by the blank canvas, do not fear! Bookbinding is art with rules! Follow the directions and something will appear at the end.

The books in this section can serve any number of purposes. There is a form for many uses, be it journal or watercolor, for personal use, or a gift.

Here are some things to think about when choosing a book structure:

- What will it be used for? Journaling? Sketching? Painting? What kind of paper is good for that activity?
- Can that paper fold? Try tacketed.
- Is it used in single sheets? Make a sketchbook.
- Does it need to open flat? Make a Friend of a Friend book.
- How big will it be? Does it need to fit in a pocket or a backpack? All the books can be customized to any specification. The only limit is the size of the paper.

- How thick will it be? How many pages are needed? Some structures work better with thick books (tacketed), others with thin (sketchbook).
- Is the sewing part of the decoration? Can embellishments be added there?
- What will the covering material be?

Tacketed Book

STUDIO PROJECT

This book is a modern variation on an ancient structure that goes back to the first century CE. Tackets were the original staples, made out of twisted leather or vellum. The tacketed binding is a flexible, easily altered structure. These bindings are often seen with a leather wrapper, visible sewing, and guard tabs. The wrapper encompasses the textblock, providing added protection to this soft-bound structure.

It is easy to alter the tacket placement to create designs on the spine. You can use beads, buttons, and other embellishments to emphasize the sewing. Add a closure to the wrapper to wrap this package with style.

SIZE
6" × 5" (15 × 12.5 cm)

TIME
Time: approx. 1 hour
Prep: 30 minutes
Make: 20 minutes
Downtime/Drying time: None

TOOLS
• Bone folder
• Awl or pin vise
• Needle
• Knife
• Scissors
• Beeswax
• Punching trough
• Needle
• Masking tape

OPTIONAL TOOLS
• 90-degree triangle

MATERIALS
• **Textblock:** Thick sections are good here, as this will emphasize the tackets and provide enough space between the sections so that there is less stress on the covering material.

• For this model, we used five 8-folio sections of text-weight paper, cut, pressed, and trimmed to 6" × 5" (15 × 12.5 cm).

• 1 piece of heavy stock or handmade paper, cut to the height of the textblock and 2½ × the width of the textblock + 1 thickness of the textblock.

This should be enough to wrap all the way around the textblock, plus make an additional flap on the front cover. For this model, we used a 6" × 13" (15 × 33 cm) piece.

• Linen or hemp thread

• 1 piece of .010 pt. stock or other waste paper for the punching template, cut to the height of the textblock and the width of the thickness of the textblock in a relaxed state. Give the sections some room to expand. For this model, we used a 6" × ¾" (15 × 2 cm) piece.

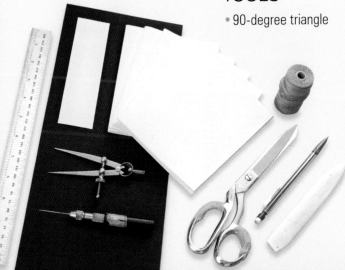

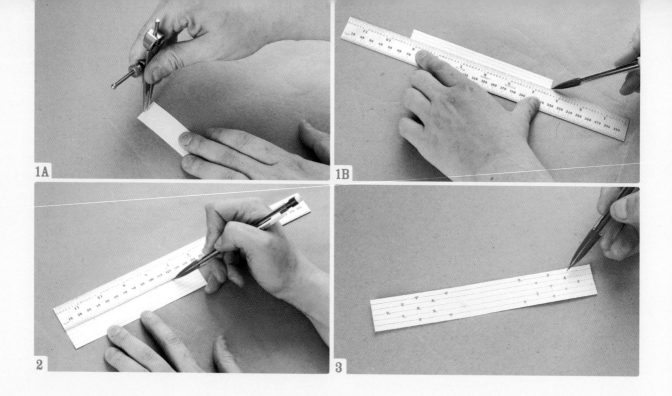

1A

1B

2

3

The sewing for this book is done in pairs of holes. The pairs for each section are in different places along the spine so as not to rip the cover material from the stress of attaching the sections to the cover. If you would like to adjust these instructions to make a small book, make tackets near the head and tail. For a larger book, add sewing stations in the middle.

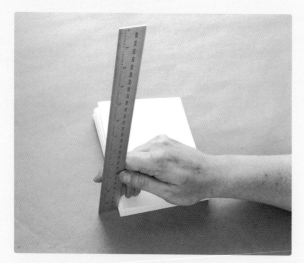

To measure the thickness of the textblock, apply a medium amount of pressure so there is some room for the pages to expand. Take a measurement across the spine.

INSTRUCTIONS

Make the Punching Template

1. Use dividers to segment the width of the template by the number of sections minus one. For this model, we have 7 sections, so the width is 6. Mark this measurement at both ends of the template and connect the lines.

2. Divide the height of the template into an even number of segments about ½" (1.5 cm) apart. For this model, we used 14 segments.

3. Choose any pattern of pairs of marks along the height that is pleasing to you. For this model, we marked as follows: On the first and last lines, we marked at 3, 5, 12, and 14; on the second and fourth lines, we marked at 2, 4, 10, and 13. We marked the center line at 1, 3, 12, and 14.

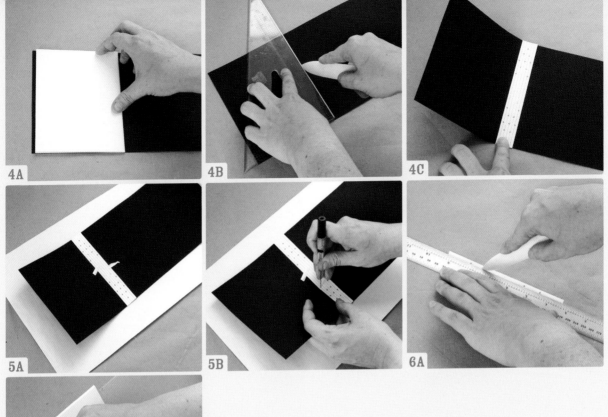

4A

4B

4C

5A

5B

6A

6B

Mark and Score the Wrapper

4. Measuring in from one side of heavy stock, mark for the width of the textblock, plus a small amount (1/16" [2 mm]), so there will be a very small overhang on the fore edge of the textblock. Score and fold to this mark, being sure to align the bottom edges to keep it square. Beyond the first crease mark, crease and fold the thickness of the textblock (i.e., the width of the punching template).

Punch the Sewing Stations into the Wrapper

5. The sewing stations on the sections need to match up with the sewing stations on the wrapper. Align the punching template between the folds of the wrapper that mark the spine width. Lightly tape the template down. Using a pin vise or awl, punch holes through the template to create the same sewing pattern on the wrapper. Remove the template.

6. With the bone folder, score along the first line of the punching template to make it easier to use in the punching trough. Open the first section and place it in the punching trough. Place the template into the fold of the section and punch holes at the marked points. Continue to punch each section, scoring the next line of the punching template.

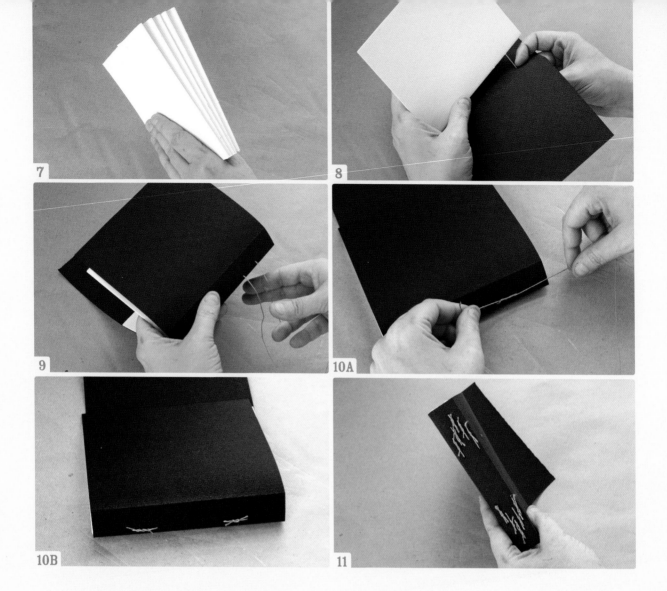

Sew the Book

7. Decide whether you want the knots to appear on the inside or the outside of the book.

8. Begin with the first section and work in the first row of punched holes on the spine of the wrapper. To have the knots on the outside, start from the outside of the wrapper, sew through the first sewing station of the wrapper and through the first section of the textblock, and leave a 3" (7.5 cm) tail.

9. Bring the needle back through the textblock at the next sewing station, bringing the thread to the outside of the wrapper.

10. Make a knot with the tail of the thread. Cut the tails. Repeat for the other pair of holes in the section.

11. Continue to add sections inside the wrapper, sewing in pairs.

13A 13B
14A 14B

Make the Flap in the Wrapper

12. Close the wrapper around the textblock.

13. Mark 1/16" (2 mm) beyond the fore edge of the textblock. Score this line. Hint: If the book is intended to hold added items, such as photos, make the fore edge score the same width as the spine.

14. Hold the textblock and wrapper with the spine up. Mark the thickness of the fore edge. Score this point.

15. Wrap the wrapper around the textblock.

Consider adding a closure, such as a button and tie, a tie alone, or a loop and clasp.

15

Friend-of-a-Friend
Book

The Friend-of-a-Friend binding is a wonderful binding that allows access to each page all the way into the gutter. It opens completely flat for full use of each and every page. This structure is good for small albums, guest books, and cookbooks, and it's great for sketchbooks. The ingenious spine attachment allows the hinging mechanism to function unhindered, meaning ... *it opens flat*! This structure can be sewn fairly quickly. The sewing method keeps the sections together along the entirety of the spine, while aiding in the opening of the sections when the book is in use. The covers and the textblock are the exact same size and the covers are sewn on at the same time as the textblock.

This book is named Friend-of-a-Friend because Stacie learned it from her friend, who learned it from its creator, Gary Frost (inventor of the sewn board binding), who developed it as a conservation technique. Stacie then taught it to Amy.

SIZE
7" × 5" (17.5 × 12.5 cm)

TIME
Time: approx. 2 hours
Prep: 20 minutes
Make: 1½ hours
Downtime/Drying time: preferably overnight, but not super important

TOOLS
- Bone folder
- Sewing needle
- Scissors
- Glue brush
- Ruler
- Awl
- Pencil
- Small or large mat knife

OPTIONAL TOOLS
- Punching trough

MATERIALS
- 12 folded, 4-folio sections of paper with a final trim of 7" × 5" (18 × 13 cm)
- Cover board: .020 pt. or light card/folder stock, folded in 2 single-folio sections, with a final trim of 7" × 5" (18 × 13 cm)
- 2 pieces of light card/folder stock (.010 pt.): 1 the height of the textblock × the width of the spine of the textblock, and 1 the height of the textblock × 1¼" (3 cm), for the template
- 1 piece of book cloth, cut to the height of the textblock + turn-ins × 3 spine widths of the textblock
- 1 piece of Japanese paper, cut to the height of the textblock × 2 spine widths of the textblock
- 2 pieces of decorative paper, cut to the height of the textblock + turn-ins × 1 width of the textblock
- 25/3 thread
- Beeswax
- Waxed paper
- PVA

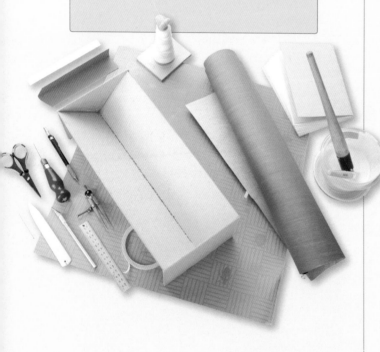

INSTRUCTIONS

Make a Punching Template

1. Cut 1 strip of .010 pt. board or waste paper to the height of the textblock and 1¼" (3 cm) wide.

2. Fold the template lengthwise. Mark a line down the center lengthwise.

3. Using dividers, divide the template into 4 equal sections along that line to make 3 sewing stations. Mark the 3 points made by the dividers.

4. At those points, mark a second point ½" (1 cm) away from what will be the tail of the book up toward the head of the book. There should now be 6 marks or 3 pairs of 2 along the center line. Mark an additional point at ¼" (6 mm) from either end of the template for the kettle stitches, totaling 8 marks.

5. Score and fold the strip of .010 pt. board along the center line.

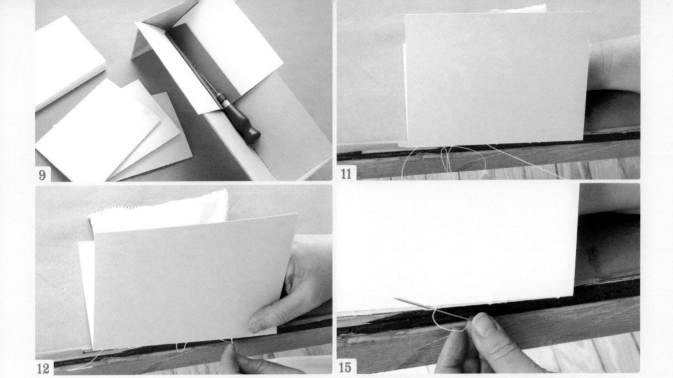

Punch the Sections

6. Keep the covers and sections in order. Open a cover to the center folio.

7. Place it in the punching trough or on the work surface. Place the .010 pt. template in the center of the fold, abutting the edge of the template to the head and tail of the section.

8. Using a pin vise or small awl, punch holes through all the pages of the section at the marks on the template.

9. Place the refolded section aside. Repeat for all the sections *and* the .020 pt. cover.

Sew the Book

10. Thread a needle with a piece of 25/3 linen. Wax the thread as desired. Position the first .020 pt. cover section of the textblock with the fold edge along the edge of the work surface. Hint: Use a light weight inside the section to hold it in place while sewing.

11. Beginning on the outside of the cover board, and working from the tail end, sew into the first hole from the outside in, run the thread along the crease, and come out through the second hole. Leave a 4" (10 cm) tail.

12. Continue working in this manner, weaving in and out of the sewing holes, until you reach the end of the cover section at the last hole. When you are finished sewing the section, take the weight out and bone down the crease of the fold. This will help the paper to absorb some of the thickness of the thread.

13. Place the next section of the text paper on top of the .020 pt. cover section.

14. Bring the needle and thread directly up into the end sewing station. Work along the inside of the section to the next sewing station. Come out of the last hole.

15. With the needle and thread on the outside of the section, link under the thread formed by sewing the previous section before going into the next sewing station so that the threads are intertwined, one hooking around the other.

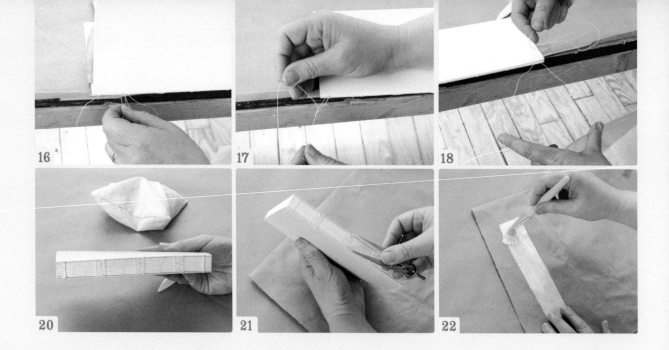

Sew the Book (continued)

16. Continue in this manner, linking under the thread of the previous section, until you reach the end of the section.

17. Tie the working thread and tail thread together (tightly) using a square knot. Add on the next section and continue sewing along the section, linking into the thread of the section below.

18. At the end of the third section, work a kettle stitch: Bring the thread between the first and second sections and loop around the end thread, making a circle of thread. Come up through the circle and pull tightly. This will make a diagonal stitch between the sections. Do this at the end of every section.

19. Add on the next section and continue sewing, making sure to link under the previous section's thread, and forming a kettle stitch at the end of each section.

20. Continue in this manner until the entire textblock is sewn, including the second .020 pt. cover, ending with 2 kettle stitches, one on top of the other. Cut the thread, leaving a 1" (2.5 cm) tail.

Prepare the Spine

21. Cut a strip of Japanese paper that is the height of the textblock and 2× the width of the textblock's sewn spine. Use dividers to measure this.

22. On a piece of waste paper glue out the Japanese paper.

23. Center the Japanese paper along the spine and adhere it to the spine of the textblock, adhering the excess on the sides onto the .020 pt. cover boards. Rub it down with a bone folder and let it dry.

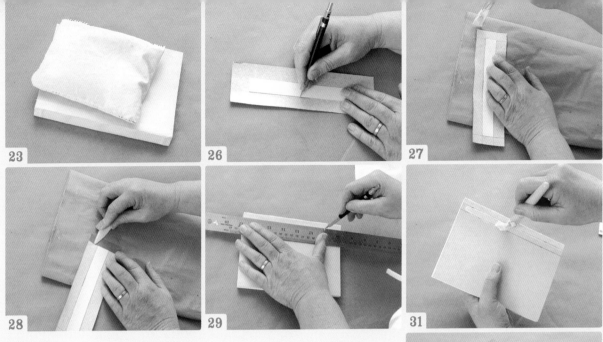

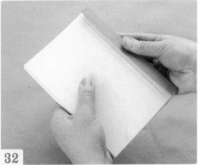

Prepare the Covering Cloth

The spine cloth is only adhered to the cover boards at the edges, so the spine remains free to move.

24. Cut 1 piece of .010 pt. board to the height of the textblock and the width of the spine of the textblock.

25. Cut 1 piece of book cloth to the height of the textblock + turn-ins (1" [2.5 cm]) and 3× the width of the spine.

26. On the glue side of the cloth, divide the cloth into 3 equal widths. Mark these lines.

27. On a piece of waste paper glue out the .010 pt. spine strip and adhere it to the center of the cloth, centering it so that there is an equal amount of excess cloth for turn-ins at the head and tail.

28. Glue up the turn-ins and fold them over.

29. Working on the outside of the textblock, mark a line that is half the width of the spine onto each cover.

30. Mark a second line the width of the spine onto each cover.

31. Being sure to not glue the section of the line that is closest to the spine, apply glue between the two lines.

32. Being sure to align the book cloth spine to the head and tail, adhere it onto the covers.

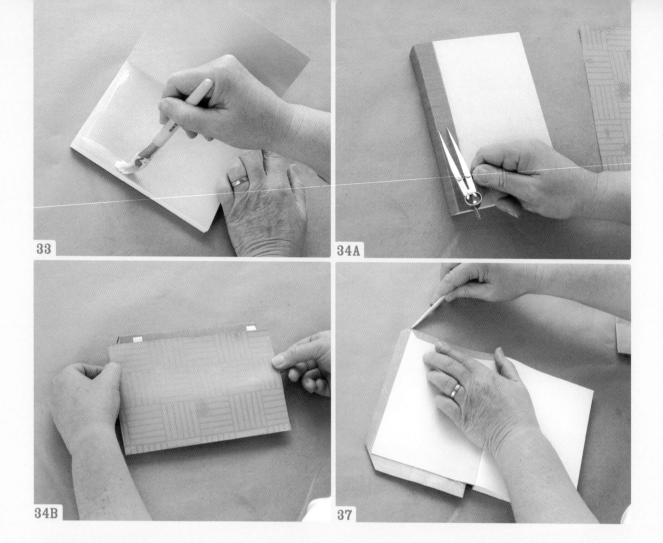

Assemble the Covers

When you are assembling the covers, you can glue
.020 pt. boards together to stiffen them, either fully or
just at the edges.

33. Cut 2 pieces of decorative paper to <u>8</u>" × 5½"
(<u>20</u> × 14 cm). This is larger than the covers to
allow for the turn-ins.

34. Use dividers to mark one-half of the book cloth
from the spine edge. **Hint:** Use low-tack tape to
mark where the paper should go.

35. Glue up the paper and adhere it to the cover,
leaving half of the cover book cloth exposed. This
paper will help to hide/cover any fraying that may
occur at the edge of the book cloth.

36. Miter the corners.

37. Glue up the turn-ins and adhere them to the inside
of the covers, head and tail first, then the fore
edge.

38. Let them dry under a weight.

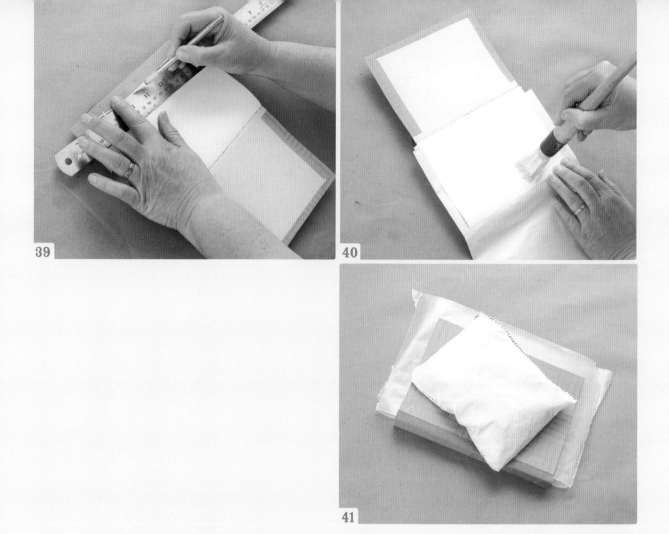

Glue Down the Pastedown

39. Put a piece of scrap board under the first and last pages of the textblock and trim 1/16" (2 mm) from the fore edge. This will compensate for any paper expansion due to the moisture in the glue.

40. Put a piece of waste paper under the first page of the textblock. Carefully glue the entire page, remove the piece of waste paper, and close the cover on top of it. Repeat for the other side. Put a piece of waxed paper under the glued sheet, between the pastedown and the first page, to act as a moisture barrier.

41. Let it dry under a weight overnight.

Sketchbook

Pick paper that best suits your style of sketchbook, be it for drawings or watercolors. Stack it up, put a cover on it, and go!

Note: This is a stab-sewn book, meaning that the sewing thread will go through the entire stack of paper at once. It will not open flat. Keep the thickness of the textblock to less than ½" (1.5 cm). Any larger and the restrictive opening will be readily apparent. It can easily be disassembled for access to the contents.

SIZE

Any size

TIME

Time: approx. 2½ hours
Prep: 30 minutes
Make: 1½ hours
Downtime/Drying time: 30 minutes or overnight

The materials required include decorative paper, glue, thread, binder's board, textblock, board papers, book cloth, hand drill, and ruler.

TOOLS

- Pencil
- Ruler
- Scissors
- Glue brush
- Hand drill
- Drill bit
- Needle
- Weight

OPTIONAL TOOLS

- Masking tape

MATERIALS

- Textblock: 1 stack of paper with a total thickness not more than ½" (1.5 cm)
- Board papers: 2 extra pieces of the textblock paper measuring ¼" (6 mm) smaller in both length and width than the cover boards **or** 2 pieces of decorative paper measuring ¼" (6 mm) smaller in both length and width than the cover boards
- 2 pieces of binder's board cut to the height of the textblock × the width of the textblock minus ¼" (6 mm); medium (.082/.087 pt.) or thick (.098 pt.) will give stability while sketching, but any thickness will do.
- Book cloth: 2 hinges cut to the height of the textblock x 1½" (4 cm), and 1 piece cut to the height of the textblock + turn-ins (1" [2.5 cm] extra) and ½ the width of the textblock + 2 board thicknesses
- 2 pieces of decorative paper cut to the length of the textblock + turn-ins (1" [3 cm] extra) and the width of the textblock; it should be enough to overlap the cloth, cover the boards, and have turn-ins at the fore edge.
- Thread
- PVA
- Waste paper
- Scrap board
- Waxed paper

INSTRUCTIONS

Assemble the Textblock

1. Stack the textblock paper and make sure all edges are aligned.

2. On either side of the textblock at the spine edge, align the book cloth hinges to the spine, with the cloth side toward the textblock and the glue side visible. **Hint:** Use a piece of masking tape to secure the cloth hinges to the first and last pages of the textblock.

3. Place the stack on the edge of the table, with the spine slightly off the edge of the table, and put a weight on it. Make sure the spine is square. **Hint:** Stack the papers between the boards for stability.

4. Apply a light coating of glue to the spine edge. This will keep the textblock aligned while the sewing stations are drilled.

Determine and Mark the Sewing Stations

5. Draw a line ¼" (6 mm) from the spine edge.

6. Mark 3 sewing stations along the spine edge of the textblock, ¼" (6 mm) in from the spine. The sewing stations are in the center, ½" (1.5 cm) in from either end. **Hint:** If the book is large, use 5 sewing stations.

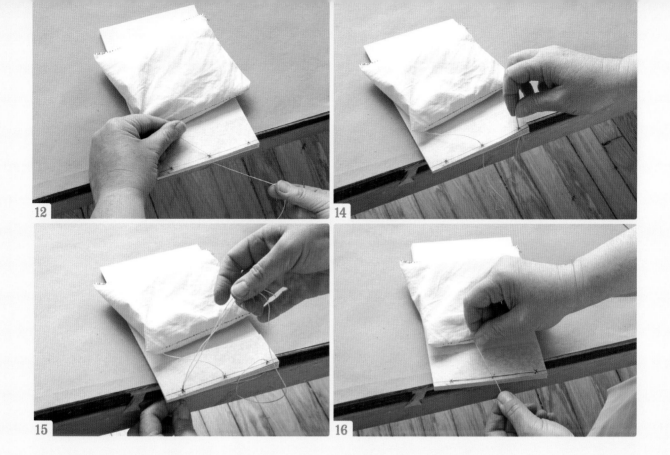

Drill the Sewing Stations

7. Put a piece of scrap board under the spine edge of the textblock. Clamp or weight it to secure all the pieces. **Hint:** Try using binder clips to secure all the pieces while drilling.

8. Move the spine edge of the textblock with the scrap board slightly off the edge of the table.

9. Put a weight on the textblock.

10. Choose the smallest drill bit that will accommodate the needle and thread you will use to sew.

11. Drill straight down at the 3 sewing station marks. Drill all the way through. Reverse the drill to get the bit out of the hole. **Hint:** Use a Dremel tool!

Sew the Textblock

Choose any thickness for your thread. It will not be seen, so don't worry about the color. The length of the thread is about 2½ × the length of the textblock.

12. Sew using the pamphlet stitch: Start at the center hole, on either side.

13. Go through to the other side, leaving a 3" to 4" (7.5 cm to 10 cm) tail.

14. Go through one of the end holes.

15. Go through the other end hole, bypassing the center.

16. Go through the center hole back to the beginning.

17. Try not to pierce the original thread, as it will be difficult to tighten. Keep the two ends of the thread on either side of the cross thread. Pull tightly, tie a square knot, and clip the ends.

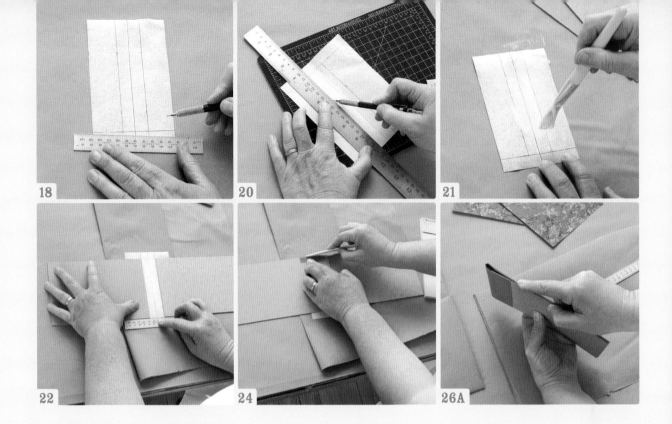

Mark the Cloth for the Cover

The cover boards will be adhered to the cover book cloth, and then attached to the textblock.

18. Mark the turn-in line across the bottom of the glue side of the book cloth (½" [1.5 cm]).

19. Mark the center of the book cloth on the glue side. Carefully fold the cloth in half lengthwise to find the center. Crease only on the top and bottom edges, so the cloth does not retain a crease mark.

20. Mark ½" (1.5 cm) on either side of the center line, and draw lines down the length of the cloth. This is where the cover boards will be adhered on the cloth. This calculation is approximately the sum of all the parts that the cloth has to cover: the measurement of the space from the spine edge to where the covers will sit on the textblock × 2 + the thickness of the textblock + the thickness of the board used. Add a little bit if the cloth you are using is thick.

Make the Cover

21. On a piece of waste paper, glue out the book cloth with an even coating of glue.

22. Align the covers to the marks that flank the center line on the cloth.

23. Make sure the cover boards are aligned with each other. **Hint:** To make sure, place a ruler along the bottom turn-in line and rest the boards on it.

24. Fold over the turn-ins, making sure the cloth is tight along the board edge.

25. Bone down the cloth on the boards. Let them dry.

Put on the Decorative Paper

26. Check to see if the book cloth is even on both boards. That is, make sure that when the cover is held closed and the fore edges are aligned, the edges of the cloth are even. If they are not, measure the edges of the cloth from the spine edge of the board and trim off the excess. The decorative paper will overlap the cloth by ⅛" (3 mm).

27. On a piece of waste paper, glue out the decorative paper.

28. Carefully place the decorative paper on the cover, overlapping the cloth by approximately ⅛" (3 mm). **Hint:** Use masking tape to mark where the paper will align over the cloth on the boards.

29. Miter the corners of the decorative paper.

30. Fold over the turn-ins, head and tail first, then the fore edge. Make sure the paper is tight along the edges of the board.

31. Bone it down. Again, make sure the paper is tight along the edges of the board.

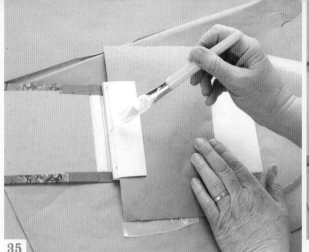

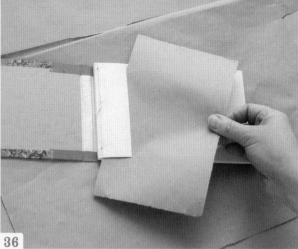

Attach the Cover to the Textblock

32. Fold the cover around the textblock, making sure to align it. Carefully place the textblock, with the cover aligned, onto your worktable.

33. Open one cover, and put a piece of waste paper under the cloth hinge.

34. Put a piece of waxed paper under the waste paper.

35. Glue out the cloth hinge. Make sure to glue straight off the hinge so that no glue gets on the decorative side of the cloth.

36. Remove the piece of waste paper. Be sure to pull it out quickly and in a straight line so that no glue gets on the decorative side of the cloth hinge.

37. Bring the cover up, over, and down onto the hinge. Make sure it is aligned with the textblock.

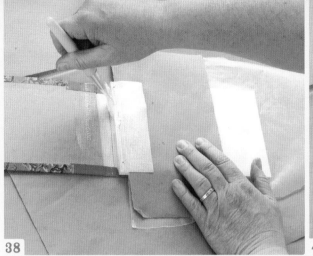

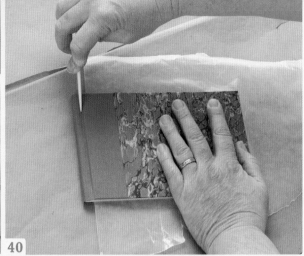

38. Quickly bone down the cover.

39. Flip the book over and repeat, applying additional glue to the spine of the textblock so that the cloth will adhere to it.

40. Bone it down along the spine, joint area, and boards, making sure everything is adhered.

41. Let the textblock dry under a weight.

Attach the Board Papers

42. On a piece of waste paper, glue out a board paper.

43. Center the board paper on the inside of one cover, and bone it down.

44. Be careful not to get any wrinkles, glue, or fingerprints on it.

45. Put a piece of waxed paper between the inside of the cover and the textblock, and close the cover.

46. Repeat with other board paper.

47. Let it dry under a weight.

Enclosures

Need an elegant way to present a book or other object? Try making a custom enclosure for it. Enclosures give a little something extra to any item.

There are other benefits to enclosures as well. They protect the book if it is fragile and should not be on a bookshelf with other books. They can help organize a group of like objects if all are housed together. And they are interesting to make!

The skills you learn in this chapter will aid you in developing hand skills for all the projects in this book, and will give you a new level of understanding when designing other personal projects. Make a jewelry box. Wrap a gift in a new and interesting way. Create a custom tool tray. Can't find a caddy to hold all those serving spoons? Make your own!

Here are some things to consider when planning your enclosure design:

- Measurements really count here. If you make the enclosure even just a little bit too small, the item will not fit (and the item should not be forced to fit in the enclosure). The object should come out easily, but not rattle around, either.

- Pick the right enclosure for the object: Is it fragile in any way? Is it for presentation?

- Can the book's design be incorporated into the enclosure?

- Additions to consider: a pull ribbon or tie; felt on the bottom tray to cushion the object; collage material.

5-Minute
STUDIO PROJECT Slipcase

The 5-Minute Slipcase is a simple enclosure that you can make quickly. This slipcase is not meant to house archival materials, as it is not strong enough, nor does it provide enough structure. It is better suited as a nice method of presentation, and there is no glue!

The slipcase may seem daunting at first, but it is not! It may not take five minutes the first time you make it, but with practice you will master the process. Careful, precision folding will help in making this a successful project.

SIZE

custom

TIME

5 minutes

TOOLS

- Bone folder
- Ruler
- Pencil

MATERIALS

- Decorative paper

The materials required include a bone folder, decorative paper, and a ruler.

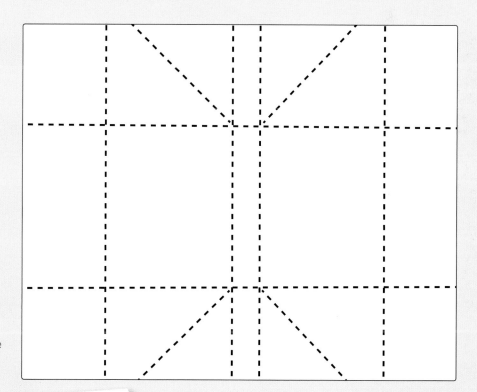

Diagram for the folds of the 5-Minute Slipcase

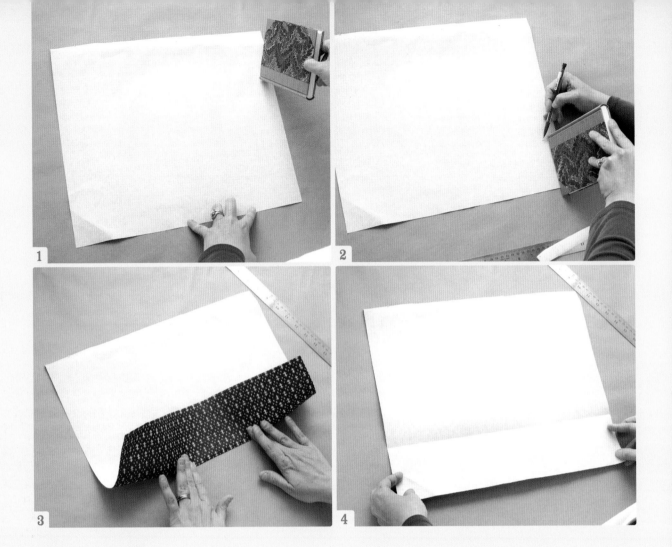

INSTRUCTIONS

Cut the Paper

1. Cut a piece of decorative paper to 4× the width of the book to be housed x the height + 2× the width – 1" (2.5 cm). **Hint:** Roll the book across the paper.

Fold the 5-Minute Slipcase

2. The first fold will be the bottom/tail edge. Working from the bottom up, measure and mark the width of the book – ½" (1.5 cm).

3. Using a bone folder, score and fold to this mark.

4. Unfold the paper.

Measure and Mark for the Height

5. Place the book on the paper, abutting the tail edge to the first fold you made. Mark along the top/head edge of the book (the height). Remove the book.

6. Using a bone folder, score and fold the paper to the height mark along the width of the paper.

7. Unfold the paper.

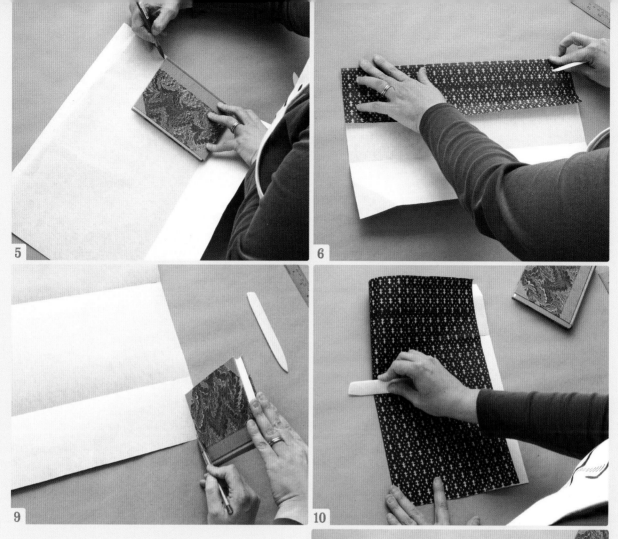

Measure and Mark for the Spine

8. Align the book to the edge of the paper and mark the thickness of the book.

9. Repeat for the lower-right corner.

10. Fold the lower paper edge over, from left to right, to meet up with the mark you just made. Fold and bone down the paper. This fold should be slightly off-center.

11. Unfold the paper and repeat on the opposite side. There should be 2 parallel folds in the center of the paper. These represent the sides of the spine.

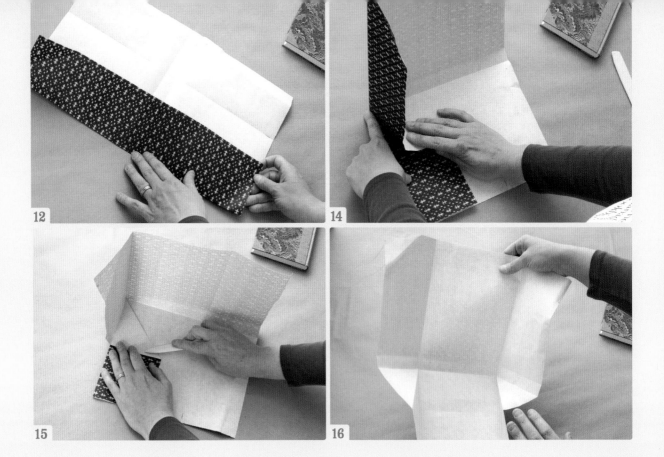

Fold the Covers In

12. With the paper open, fold along the tail fold line. The spine thickness fold should meet the height folds.

13. Using your finger or a bone folder, "pinch" the fold where it meets the spine fold.

14. Gently pivot the folded paper from that pinch point so that the spine fold meets the tail fold along the side. This will create a 45-degree fold inside the paper.

15. Bone down the paper along the inside fold.

16. Unfold the paper and repeat this fold on the 3 other corners.

17. Work with the book in the center of the paper, the fore edge on the spine crease, with the spine facing up. Bring the head and tail flaps up to the head and tail of the book. Bring the sides together. As the sides come together, the angle folds will allow the extra paper to fold nicely around the book.

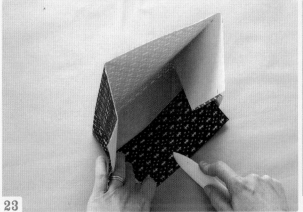

Fold the Fore Edge

18. Reassemble all of the 45-degree folds. Tuck the book inside, between the angled folds.

19. Place the paper, with the book in it, flat on your work surface.

20. Make a mark along the outer exposed edge of the book onto the decorative paper.

21. Flip the whole thing over and mark the other side the same way.

22. Remove the book.

23. Fold to the mark you just made and tuck the paper inside.

24. Flip and repeat. The second side may take a bit of finagling in order to ease the folded paper inside.

25. Place the book inside the slipcase and admire your skill and ingenuity!

Slipcase

Give a book a little extra something. Show it off. Make a slipcase for it.

This enclosure for a book is not suitable for fragile or valuable items, but it is an attractive and popular enclosure for other books. There is wear and tear as the book comes in and out of the case. The book should slide out smoothly—neither become stuck so that you have to dig it out, nor fall out swiftly.

SIZE

Custom

TIME

Time: approx. 4 hours
Prep: 30 minutes
Make: 2½ hours
Downtime/Drying time: 30 to 45 minutes total (intermittent 15- to 20-minute intervals)

TOOLS

- Ruler
- Pencil
- Mat knife
- Scissors
- Glue brushes, large and small

OPTIONAL TOOLS

- Self-healing mat
- 90-degree triangle

MATERIALS

- Linen or hemp cord
- Book cloth
- Text-weight paper
- PVA
- Waste paper
- Self-healing mat or scrap board
- .010 or .020 pt. board or folder stock
- Binder's board

INSTRUCTIONS

Measure the Book

1. Abut the ruler to the triangle to get an accurate measurement. Millimeters will count here. When in doubt, round up to the next millimeter. Stand over the book to read the ruler. Check at least two places for each measurement, as the book might not be square.

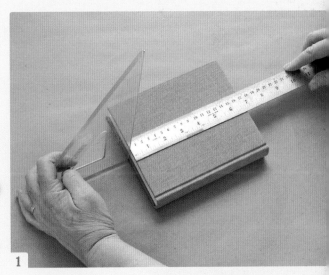

1

Measure the width, height, and thickness of the book as shown.

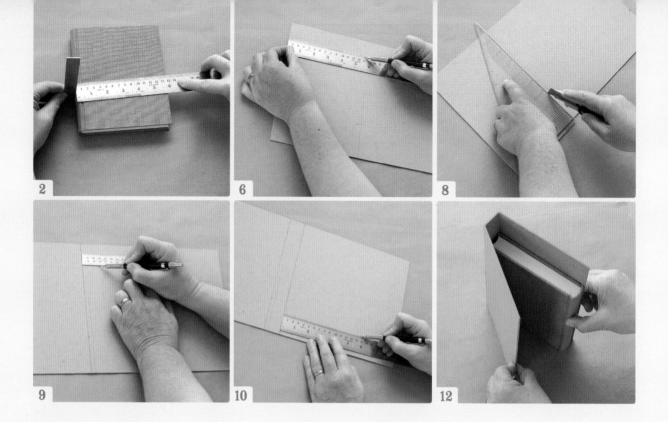

Measure the Book (continued)

2. When measuring the thickness of the book, compress it slightly and take an average measurement. Do not stress it too much or the joint can break.

3. Write down the measurements. Add 1 to 1.5 mm to the thickness measurement.

4. Choose a binder's board that is similar in thickness to the book (i.e., use thin board for a thin book, thick board for a thick book).

5. Cut a piece of binder's board, oversized, and with the grain going in the direction of the height measurement. The board should be larger than the book by the height + 1 thickness, and by 2 widths and 3 thicknesses. It should be enough to wrap around the book and the head and tail pieces. Make sure the board is square.

Score the Board

6. Measure and mark the width of the book on the board.

7. Align a straightedge or triangle to the mark.

8. Holding the straightedge steady, make repeated shallow cuts with the mat knife. Make several cuts. Cut until the board bends easily. **Caution:** Try not to go through the board completely, because it needs to bend, not be cut. It is okay if the cuts go through in spots.

9. From that score line measure, mark, and score the thickness measurement (the original plus the 1 to 1.5 mm).

10. From the thickness measurement, measure and mark the width measurement.

11. Cut off any excess board.

12. Wrap the board around the book to make sure it fits.

Cut the Head and Tail Pieces

13. From the excess board, cut 2 pieces sized to the width measurement.

Line the Slipcase

14. Cut a piece of text-weight paper (it can be decorative) that is larger than the scored board, with the grain going in the direction of the length. This goes on the *inside* of the slipcase.

15. Using a big brush, glue out the paper on a piece of waste paper.

16. Put the scored board on the paper *cut side up.*

17. Bone it down well.

18. Put the lined board under a board and weight until it is dry. **Hint:** You can cover it with a piece of wax paper so that you don't get glue on it.

19. Cut 2 pieces of the same text-weight lining paper that are larger than the head and tail pieces of the board.

20. Glue out the paper and adhere the head and tail pieces. Bone them down well.

21. Put the head and tail pieces under a board and let them dry.

Determine the Length of the Case

22. Trim off the excess paper lining on all 3 pieces.

23. On one end of the head and tail pieces, cut off the point of the back corners of the board. **Caution:** Clip only the point of the corner. This will make it fit better into the case.

24. Bend the slipcase around the tail piece and see how it fits.

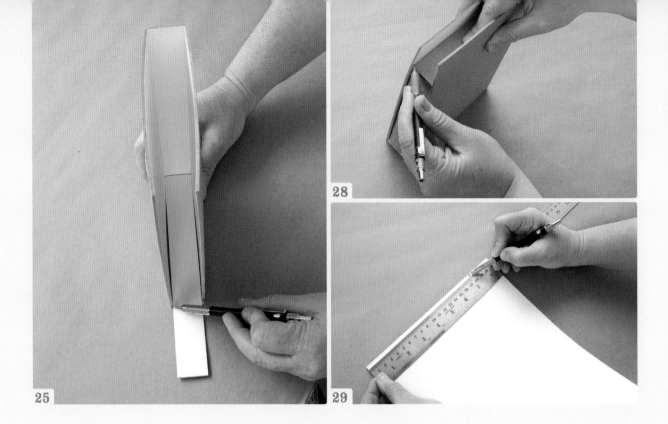

Determine the Length of the Case
(continued)

25. Mark where the tail piece meets the open sides of the slipcase. This determines the length of the tail piece.

26. Put the book in the case, on top of the tail piece. Place the head piece on top of the book and fit it into the case.

27. Mark where the head piece meets the sides of the slipcase, to determine the length.

28. On the inside of the case, mark the top edge of the head piece where it sits in the case. This will determine where the top of the case will be.

29. Add 2 millimeters to this measurement to allow for the cloth thickness and mark it. Cut off any excess board from that mark.

Assemble the Case

30. Trim the head and tail pieces to the marks you made in the process above (the length as determined by the width of the case).

31. Put a line of glue along the 3 edges of the tail piece and wrap the slipcase around it. Glue just the edge of the board; try not to get any glue on the interior of the slipcase.

32. Make sure the tail piece is as flat and even as possible against the edge of the case. **Hint:** Use your ruler to help align the tail piece in place.

33. Hold or tape the tail piece in place until the glue has adhered a bit.

34. Do the same for the head piece.

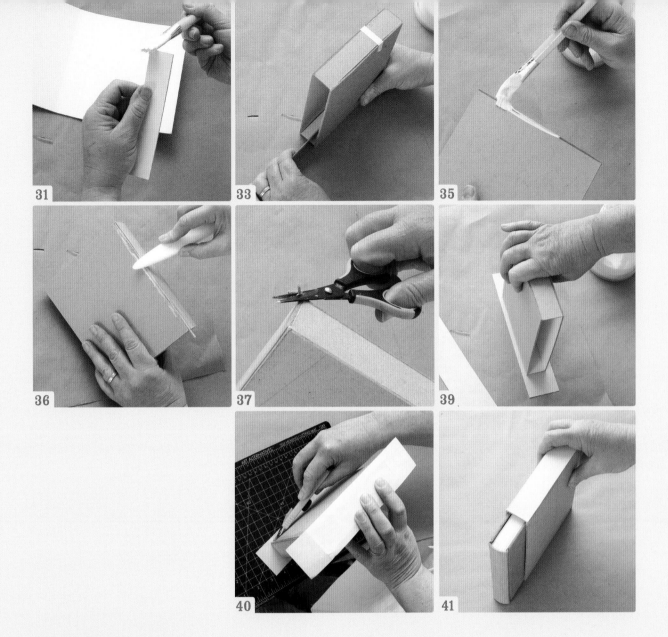

Infill the Case Joints

35. Use a piece of hemp or linen cord that is the same thickness as the board. Put a line of glue into the score lines along the length of the slipcase.

36. Adhere a piece of cord into the score lines (where the case is bending) and bone it down. This allows the covering material to bend around the corners and not rip.

37. Trim the cord to the edge of the case.

38. Cut 2 pieces of folder stock larger by at least ¼" (5 mm) than the head and tail of the slipcase.

39. Glue out the folder stock and adhere it to the top and bottom of the slipcase. This will cover any unevenness. Let it dry.

40. When it is dry, trim the folder stock to the edges of the case.

41. Put the book into the case to see if it fits.

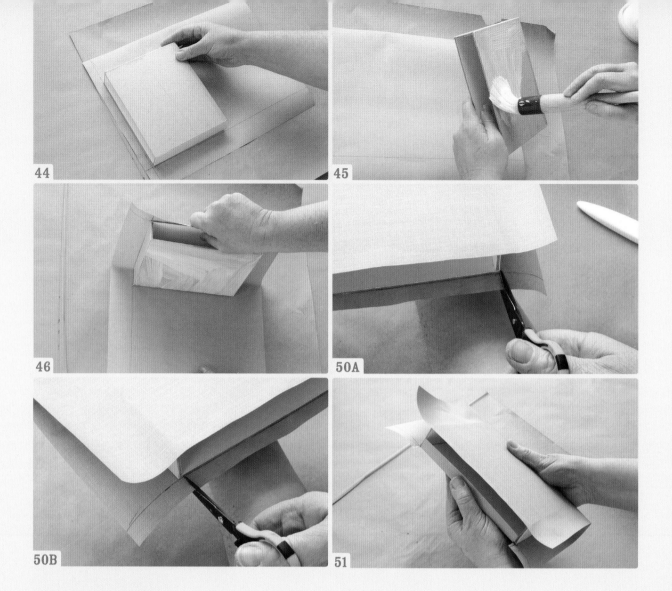

44

45

46

50A

50B

51

Cover the Slipcase

42. Cut the book cloth with the grain going lengthwise. The final height should be 2× the thickness of the case + the length, and the final width should be 2× the width of the case + the width of the case + turn-ins at both edges (about ½" [1.5 cm] total).

43. Measure and mark the turn-in (about ½" [1.5 cm]) along the height edge of the book cloth.

44. Measure and mark the thickness of the slipcase (edge to edge), plus a little bit for error; mark it along the bottom edge of the book cloth.

45. Glue out the sides of the slipcase.

46. Align the slipcase at the margin lines, with the open/fore edge side next to the mark. Roll the slipcase so that the book cloth wraps around it.

47. Make sure the cloth is tightly wrapped around the spine of the box by pushing the slipcase against the cloth, while holding the cloth.

48. Rub the cloth down to make sure the book cloth is adhered to the slipcase.

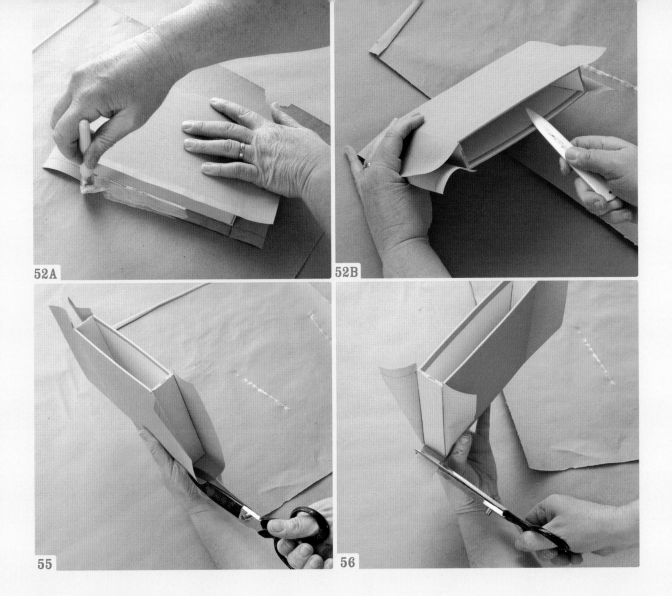

52A **52B**

55 **56**

Make the Cuts for the Folds

49. Trim the turn-ins to ½" (1.5 cm).

50. Cut the turn-ins at the head and tail of the slipcase along the line where the head and tail pieces meet the sides, at the top of the head and tail.

51. Cut tabs to cover the front edge of the head and tail pieces. These are cut from the cloth that is adhered to the sides of the slipcase and are 1 board thickness in width. The cloth should fold in cleanly.

52. Glue out the cloth, fold it in, and rub it down, making sure it is tight along the edge of the board.

53. Trim the length of the tabs so that they meet in the middle of the head and tail pieces. If they are shorter, do not trim them.

54. Glue out the tabs and rub them down. The extra material at the head and tail will overlap to cover them.

55. Make a tab at the spine end of the head and tail by cutting a line at the corners. Do not cut all the way to the board, but leave about 1 board thickness of cloth.

56. Trim the length of the tab to about ¼" (6 mm).

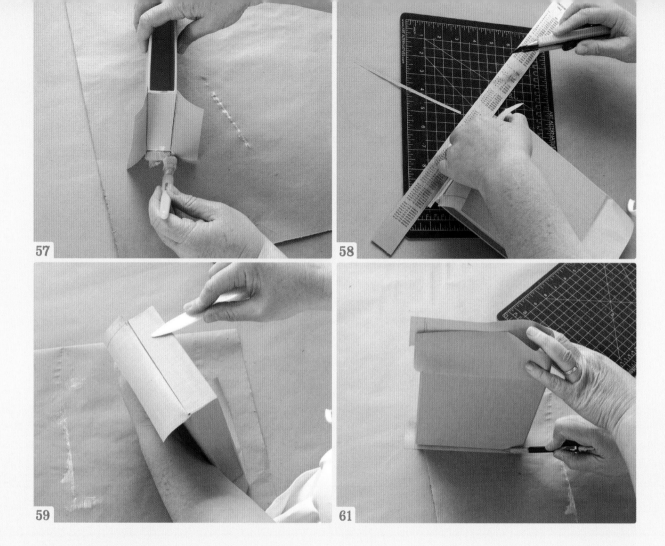

Make the Cuts for the Folds (continued)

57. Glue out the tab and turn it down to cover the spine end of the head and tail. Bone it down.

58. The sides of the head and tail cloth should overlap and stay within the borders of the head and tail. The cloth at the head and tail should not fold over onto the sides of the slipcase. Measure and trim the interior side piece to the width of the head and tail.

59. Glue out, fold, and bone down the cloth to cover the head and tail pieces.

60. Trim the length of the interior head and tail pieces to the length of the slipcase (i.e., flush at the fore edge).

61. Measure, mark, and trim the exterior head and tail pieces to the width of the slipcase.

62. Glue out, fold, and bone down the cloth to cover a second layer at the head and tail.

63. The tab at the fore edge (open edge) folds in to cover the front of the head and tail board. Trim the tab to ½" (1.5 cm) in length.

64. Trim the tab further by making an angled cut from the corners of the slipcase. Make this cut about 1 board thickness in length.

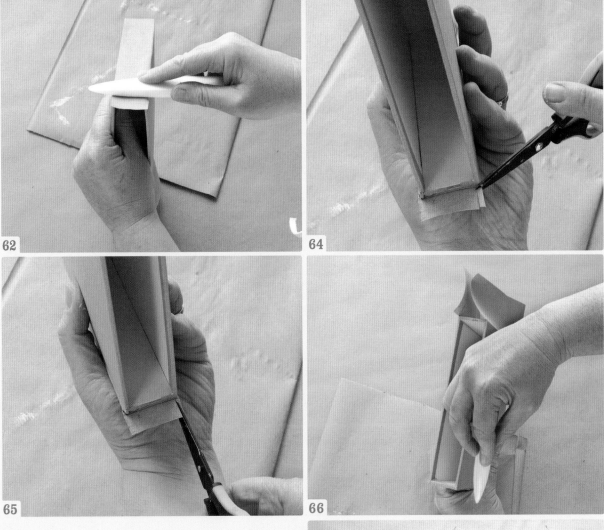

62

64

65

66

65. Continue the trim as a straight cut so that the tab fits within the thickness of the slipcase and the angled cut covers the tabs that overlap the board.

66. Glue out the tab, fold it in, and rub it down.

67. Repeat for the other side. Allow it to dry.

68. Let the entire slipcase dry so that any glue on the inside is no longer sticky (about 1 hour). Put the book in the slipcase with a board and weight on it and allow it to dry completely.

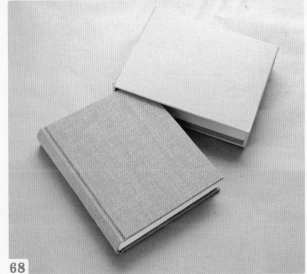

68

Suggestion: Try using two colors of cloth or a decorative paper, or adding a pull ribbon.

French Box

The French Box provides a sturdy, attractive housing for books or other materials. The construction allows for easy access to the item, as the walls are not solid. You can easily modify the French Box to hold any item, such as a deck of cards, note cards, or jewelry.

SIZE

6" × 5" × 1"
(15 × 12.5 × 2.5 cm)
to house a tacketed book

TIME

Time: approx. 1½ hours
Prep: 30 minutes
Make: 1 hour
Downtime/Drying time: preferably overnight

TOOLS

• Bone folder
• Ruler
• Knife
• Glue brush
• Weights

MATERIALS

• Book cloth
• Decorative paper
• Binder's board
• Ribbon (optional)
• Waste paper
• PVA

INSTRUCTIONS

Measure Twice

1. Measure the item that is going to be boxed. Make note of the height, width, and thickness.

Make the Base

2. Cut a piece of mat board to the height and width of the object.

3. Cut a piece of decorative paper to the size of the mat board plus turn-ins of ⅜" (1 cm) on all sizes.

4. Glue out the decorative paper and adhere it to the base board and miter the corners.

5. Wrap the excess around the board and adhere it to the bottom.

Suggestion: Try adding a ribbon to tie the box shut. If you do, the ribbon would go under the interior decorative paper and under the tray.

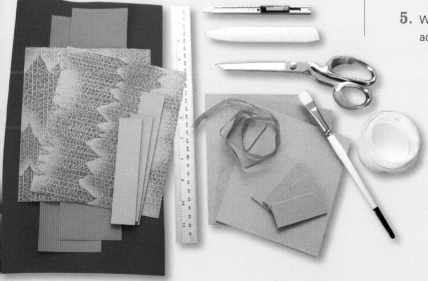

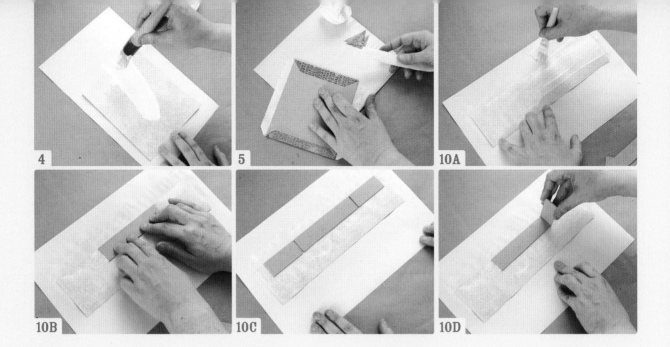

Make the Walls

The walls will wrap around the base. The walls do not form a solid ring around the base, but there is an opening to lift the book out.

6. Cut 2 long strips of board to the thickness of the object + 1 board thickness (about ¼" [6 mm]). The total combined board width should be 4 to 5× the width of the base board. The walls sit next to the base board, not on top of it. The walls should end up level with the thickness of the book as it sits on the base.

7. From these 2 long strips, cut 4 pieces to the same width as the base board.

8. Cut 2 of these strips in half (to make 6 pieces total); 2 strips will be equivalent to the width of the base board, and 4 strips will be equivalent to half the width of the base board.

Cut the Cloth for the Walls

9. One piece of cloth covers both faces of the wall boards and attaches the walls to the base. The cloth should be 2× the width of the base board + ½" (1.5 cm), and be 3× the length of the wall boards. Cut 2 pieces.

Glue the Walls

10. Working on a piece of waste paper, glue out two-thirds of the cloth lengthwise. Place the full-width wall board along the glued edge and in the center of the cloth widthwise. Leaving one board thickness on either side of the center board, glue the half-boards next to the center board, also flush to the edge. **Hint:** Place the board edge flush on the book cloth and then "tip" it over onto the glued cloth. This will ensure that it is one board thickness away and will fold around to make a sharp corner.

Cut and Glue the Cloth to Wrap around the Walls

11. Cut from the edge of the cloth to the upper corner of the board.

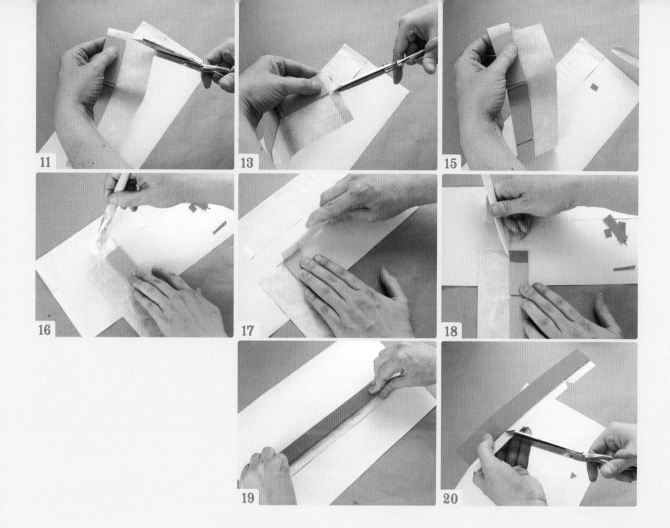

12. Move the ruler to the edge of the cloth, and cut the cloth to wrap around the walls.

13. Move one board thickness out from the previous cut, and make a parallel cut starting and stopping at the same places.

14. Place a ruler 90 degrees flush with the top long edges of the glued-down boards. Make a cut starting from the outermost parallel cut and extending to the edge of the cloth (about ¼" [6 mm]), being careful not to cut all the way to the corner of the board.

15. Carefully snip between the two parallel cuts about ½" (1.5 cm) away from the corner of the board.

16. Glue out the remainder of the cloth, including the tabs on the edges.

17. Gingerly fold the glued tabs onto the boards, being careful to not get glue on the cloth.

18. Glue the little tab along the top edge of the board.

19. Flip the glued boards and cloth over onto the remaining glued cloth, pulling the cloth so that it is taut. Apply more glue if needed. Bone it down. The boards should now be completely covered, with an extra strip of cloth sticking up that is not glued down.

20. Lay the long strip of cloth so that it is flat, with the excess cloth facing down. Being careful not to take off too much, remove a triangle of cloth from beneath each spot where the boards meet.

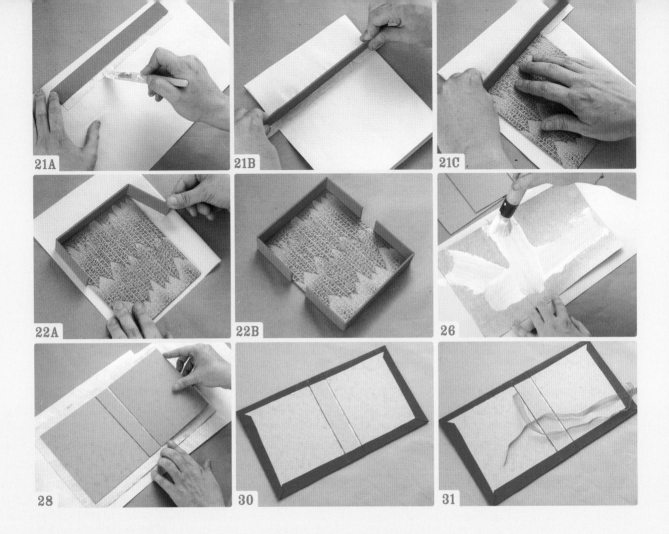

21A   21B   21C

22A   22B   26

28   30   31

Cut and Glue the Cloth to Wrap around the Walls (continued)

21. Gingerly glue up the remaining exposed book cloth. Bring up the cloth-covered walls so that the base of the walls is glued onto the exposed cloth. Working from the center out, carefully place the base board on the glued cloth, aligning it to the center wall. Press down to adhere the cloth to the underside of the base board.

22. Working with the half-width side walls, carefully angle them in to the base board and tuck the glued cloth underneath. Press down firmly to adhere. This may be a little bit awkward; work carefully and quickly, adding more glue as needed. Repeat to adhere the other walls to the base board.

Make the Case

The lid should cover the tray completely.

23. Cut 2 pieces of board to the width of the base board + 3 board thicknesses × the height of the base board + 4 board thicknesses. These will be the front and back covers of the case.

24. Cut 1 piece of board to the height of the front and back board covers × the wall height + 1 board thickness. This will be the spine strip.

25. Cut 1 piece of decorative paper or book cloth 2× the width of the case boards + 1 spine strip width + ¾" (2 cm) × the height of the case boards + ¾" (2 cm).

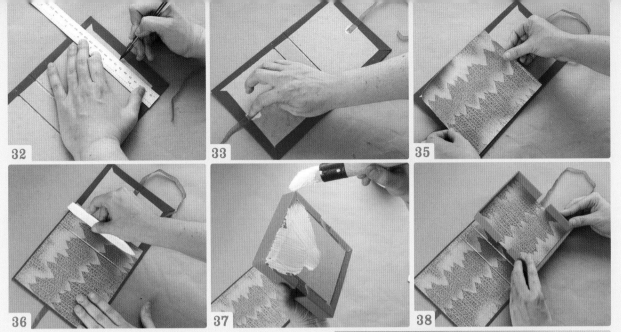

Glue Up the Case

26. Glue out the entire piece of cover book cloth.

27. Working quickly, center the spine strip on the book cloth and glue it down.

28. Place a cover board on either side of the spine strip, leaving a space of 1 board thickness between the spine and boards, and being careful to align the bottom edges of all 3 pieces.

29. Flip it over and bone it down.

30. Flip it again, trim back the corners, and glue down the turn-ins.

31. Cut 2 ribbons to 8" (20 cm).

32. Measure the height of the covers to find the center, and mark it.

33. Use a little bit of glue to adhere the ends of the ribbons to the case.

34. Cut a piece of decorative paper to just a bit shorter than the height of the case, and wide enough to cover one board, across the spine and slightly onto the other board.

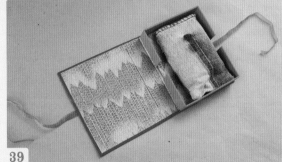

35. Glue out the decorative paper and carefully align it to an edge of the interior of the case.

36. Adhere the paper across the case cover, working it into the joint along the spine, across the spine, and into the second joint and onto the second board slightly. Bone it down. Let it dry.

37. Carefully glue up the bottom/underside of the completed tray. Lift your brush up on the edges so as not to get glue along the sides of the tray.

38. Place the tray on the exposed side of the case, aligning it with the spine joint on the inside edge.

39. Place some scrap board and weights inside the adhered tray and leave it to sit overnight.

Advanced
Projects

These projects build on the skills you learned in the previous chapters. They also introduce new concepts to stretch your skill level. Book in a Box brings basic enclosure concepts to altered books. Limp Paper incorporates all of the measuring and folding skills you've learned thus far to create a new take on traditional sewing on tapes. And Travel Journal combines tackets and the folding skills of the 5-Minute Slipcase to create a book that is ready for an adventure.

STUDIO PROJECT

Limp Paper

This simple variant on a traditional Limp Vellum binding provides a sturdy housing for a textblock and a wealth of possibilities for adornment. The structure is easy enough to vary to all tastes and needs. Add a few tapes, alter the covers, weave things together more or less, and so on. By gluing the heavy cover stock turn-ins, you will give the book a bit more stability.

This project introduces a technique for sewing on a support system: linen tapes. The linen tapes provide something for the textblock to hold on to. More advanced bookbinding techniques use supported sewing, such as linen tapes or cords. This is a great project to practice on if you want to become familiar with this type of structure.

SIZE

7" × 5" (17.5 × 12.5 cm)

TIME

Time: approx. 1½ hours
Prep: 20 minutes
Make: 1 hour
Downtime/Drying time: Overnight

TOOLS

- Bone folder
- Needle

- Scissors
- Knife
- Punching trough
- Awl or pin vise
- Glue brush
- Beeswax
- Masking tape
- Weight

OPTIONAL TOOLS

- Chisel

MATERIALS

- Ten 4-folio sections of textblock paper that has been cut, folded, pressed, and trimmed to 7" × 5" (17.5 × 12.5 cm)
- 1 piece of stiff paper, such as a handmade paper, sized to 9¼" × 12½" (23 × 32 cm), approximately 1" (2.5 cm) larger than the textblock
- 3 strips of thin linen tape, leather, or ribbon cut to 5" × 2" (12.5 × 5 cm), approximately the thickness of the textblock plus enough to easily thread through the cover
- 25/3 linen thread
- Japanese paper cut to 7" × 1¼" (17.5 × 3 cm), the spine thickness of the textblock × the height of the textblock
- PVA
- Waste paper

INSTRUCTIONS

Make a Punching Template (See page 32.)

1. Cut 1 strip of 0.10 pt. board or waste paper to the height of the textblock and 1¼" (3 cm) wide.

2. Mark a line down the center lengthwise. Along that line, use dividers to mark 3 equidistant points by walking the dividers 4 times. Mark those points.

3. Continuing to work along the center line, mark 1 point ¼" (6 mm) away from each of the 3 divider marks from the tail to the head of the book. These marks are very slightly wider than the width of the linen sewing tapes. When sewn, the thread should lie flat over the tapes, going over them easily and not piercing through them. The tapes should not bunch or be restricted at all.

4. Mark ½" (1 cm) in from either end. These last 2 sewing stations will be for kettle stitches.

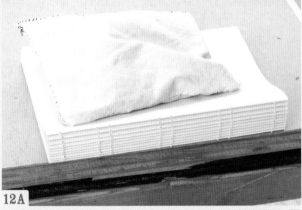

12A

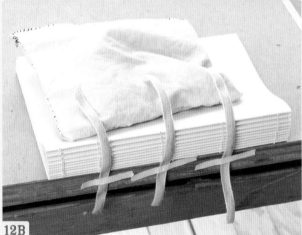

12B

Punch the Sections

5. Open a collated section to the center folio.

6. Place it in the punching trough, abutting it to one side.

7. Place the .010 pt. template on the inside of the section, also abutting it to the side, making sure all are aligned.

8. Using a pin vise or small awl, punch holes through all of the pages of the section as marked on the punching template.

9. Remove both the punching template and the section, and place the refolded section aside.

10. Repeat for all sections.

Sew the Book

11. Thread a needle with a piece of 25/3 linen thread. Wax the thread as desired.

12. Place the textblock along the edge of a press board at the edge of your table, and weight it. Center the sewing tapes to their corresponding sewing stations and tape them to the press board.

13. Beginning on the outside of the section, and working from the tail end, sew into the first hole, run the thread along the crease, and come out the second hole. Leave a 4" (10 cm) tail. **Hint:** Place a small weight inside the section as you sew it. Remember to take it out when you sew the end of the section, *before* boning it down and sewing the kettle stitch.

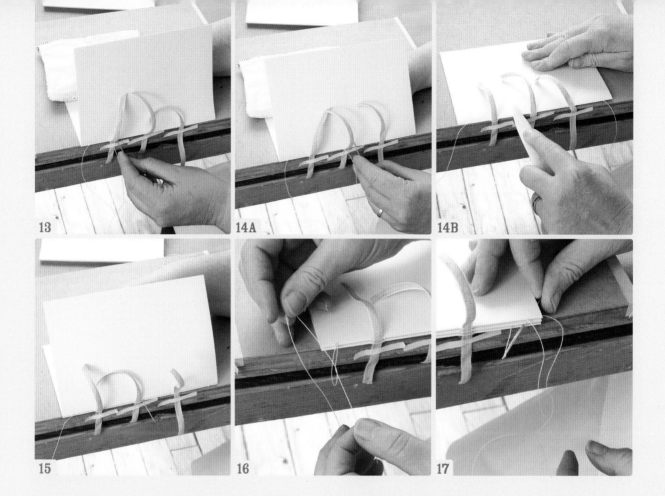

14. Bring the thread around the outside of the sewing tape and return it to the center of the section. Continue working in this manner, weaving in and out of the sewing stations and around the tapes, until you reach the end of the section. At the end of the section, bone down the crease of the fold. This will help the paper to absorb some of the thickness of the thread.

15. Place the next section on top of the sewn section. Bring the needle and thread directly up into the sewing station. Work along the inside of the section to the next sewing station.

16. Tie the working thread and tail thread together (tightly) using a square knot. Add on the next section and continue sewing along that section, working around the tapes.

17. At the end of the third section, work a kettle stitch: Bring the thread between the first and second sections, loop it around the end thread, and come up through the working thread, making a knot. Do this at the end of every section.

18. Add on the next section and continue sewing, making sure to form a kettle stitch at the end of each section, and boning down each section.

19. Continue in this manner until the entire text block is sewn, ending with 2 kettle stitches, one on top of the other. Cut the thread, leaving a 1" (2.5 cm) tail.

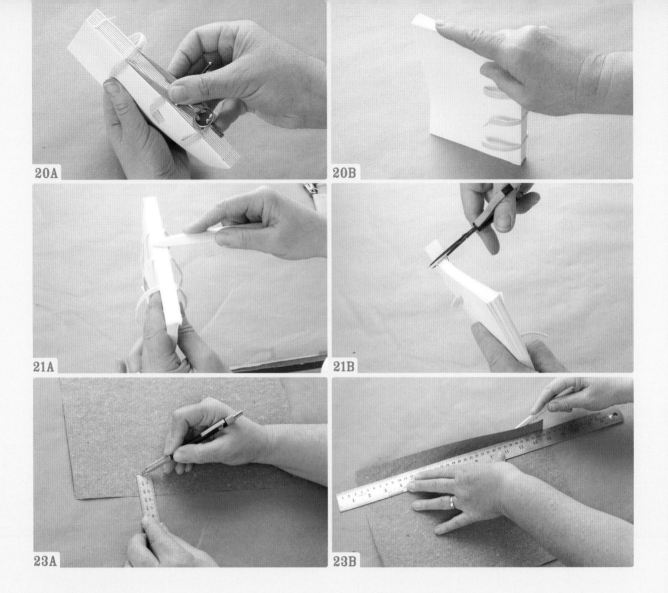

20A

20B

21A

21B

23A

23B

Line the Spine

20. Cut 1 piece of Japanese paper to the width of the spine and oversized in length. For the width of the textblock, measure edge to edge across the spine from the first to the last section. Gently tap the head, tail, and spine edges of the textblock on the table to make sure all the sections of the textblock are aligned and square.

21. Glue up the spine and apply some Japanese paper, being sure to work it into the spine. Make sure the entire length is adhered. Set it aside and let it dry with a weight on it. When it's dry, trim the length to the head and tail of the textblock.

Make the Cover

22. Make preliminary cover folds using heavy cover stock. The head and tail edges of the cover should be the same height as the textblock or *very* slightly larger.

23. Measure 1½" (4 cm) from the bottom edge of the paper. Score and fold. Open the fold.

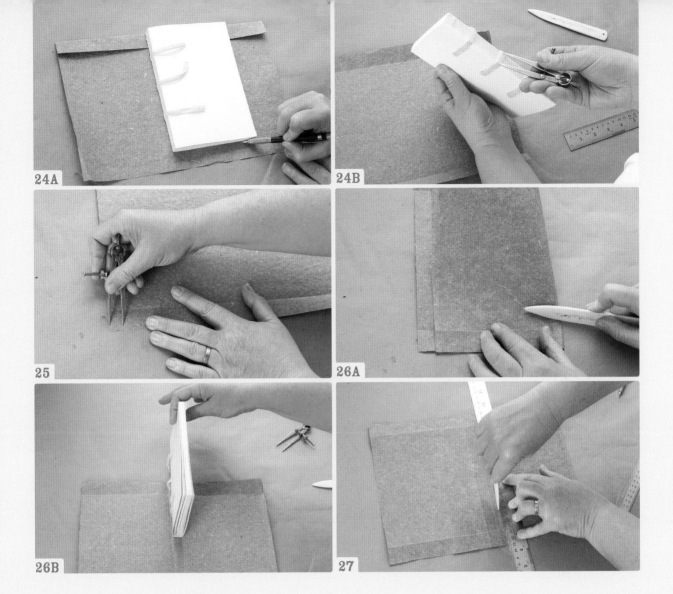

24A

24B

25

26A

26B

27

24. Measure 1½" (4 cm) from the top edge of the paper. Score and fold. Open the fold.

25. Measure the width of the spine. Use this measurement to make a mark in from either side edge of the paper. Measure from one edge to the other edge of the first and last sections of the textblock. Dividers are useful here.

26. Bring the paper over to meet up with the mark you just made, and fold the paper. Unfold the paper and repeat for the opposite side. These folds establish the spine. Unfold the paper.

27. With the cover stock open, and the right side facing up, measure ¼" (7 mm) out from each spine fold. Score and *do not fold*. This is the joint line.

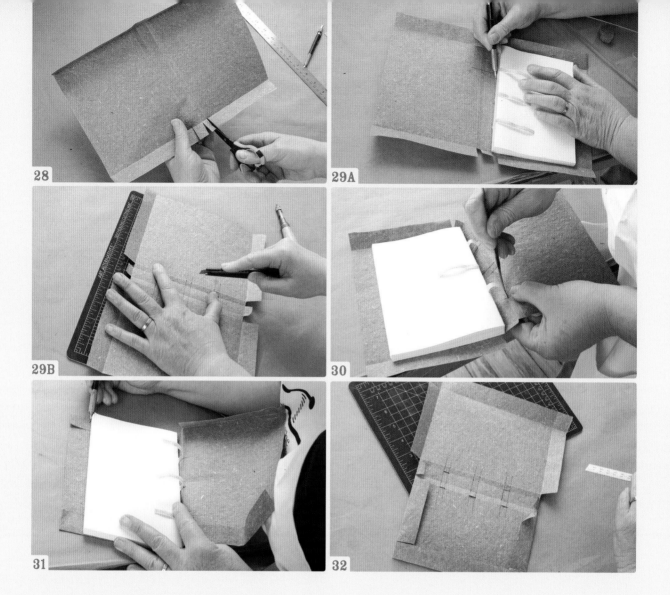

28. Remove the upper and lower spine folds, up to the head and tail folds, but leave a "tongue" in the center. Cut from the edge of the paper to the head and tail fold line. Cut across the fold line to remove the paper in the joint space. You can trim the tab that is created in the spine area so that it does not interfere with the tapes when the book is assembled.

29. Flip the cover stock and place the textblock within the spine folds. Mark where the tapes fall on either side along the spine folds, and again along the ¼" (6 mm) joint score. Cut slits along these marks.

30. Lace the tapes out through the cover stock and back in. Make sure the spine of the textblock is flush with the cover stock.

31. With the textblock in the cover, make a mark ⅛" (3 mm) beyond the textblock on the excess cover. Repeat for the opposite side. Take the textblock out of the cover.

32. Score and fold along the fore edge mark.

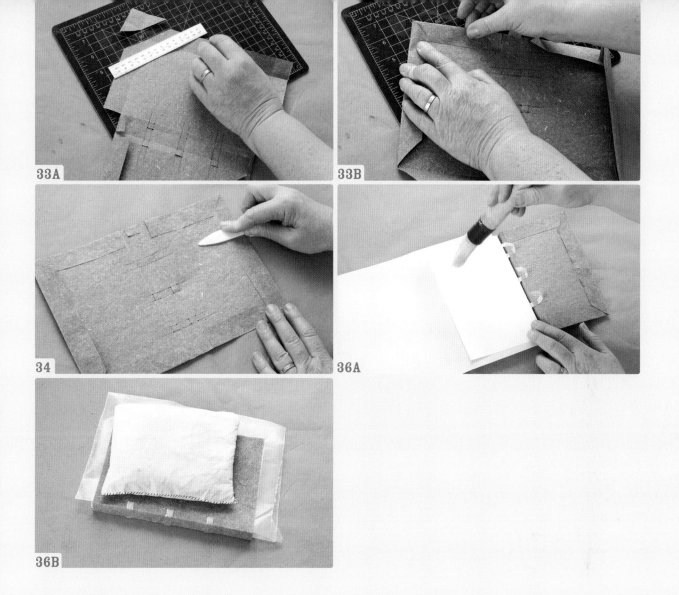

Cut the Corners

33. Use a ruler to cut off a triangular corner at the point where the head and tail folds meet the fore edge fold. When folded, the edges should meet.

34. Glue down the turn-ins, being sure to bone them down heavily. With the heavy stock it may take a bit more effort to get the paper to adhere to itself. Glue down the spine tabs.

35. Place the textblock in the cover and lace the tapes through the slots.

Glue the Pastedown

36. Glue the first sheet of paper with a piece of waste paper underneath. Take the piece of waste paper straight out and close the cover onto the glued-out page. Put waxed paper between pastedown and the textblock. Repeat for the back of the book. This leaf will ensure that the tapes do not shift. Place the book under a weight to dry overnight.

STUDIO PROJECT

Travel Journal

Off on an adventure? This book fits into a pocket or bag, and has everything you'll need: paper, pen, and pockets for memorabilia, all in one tidy package. It has one large section as the textblock, two pockets, a pen loop, and a flap with a button closure.

SIZE

6½" × 4" (16 × 10 cm)

TIME

Time: approx. 4 hours
Prep: 45 minutes
Make: 2 hours
Downtime/Drying time:
30 minutes plus pressing time for the textblock

TOOLS

- Knife
- Ruler
- Needle

- Glue brush
- Pencil
- Eraser
- Bone folder
- Small scissors
- Awl
- Self-healing mat or scrap board to cut on
- Weight

OPTIONAL TOOLS

- Punching trough
- 90-degree triangle

MATERIALS

- 24 sheets of text-weight paper, roughly cut to 6½" × 8¼" (16 × 21 cm)
- 2 pieces of .010 or .020 pt. map/folder stock (light card stock) for covers, cut to 6½" × 4" (16 x 10 cm)
- 5 pieces of book cloth: 1 cut to approximately 12" × 9" (30.5 × 23 cm), 2 pieces for tabs cut to 2" × 1" (5 × 2.5 cm), and

- 1 piece for the spine cut to 6½" × 2" (16 × 5 cm)
- 18/3 unwaxed linen thread
- Thin pen
- Flat button
- 2 pieces of heavy-weight paper for the pockets, cut to 7" × 8" (17.5 × 20 cm)
- PVA
- Waste paper
- Ribbon

INSTRUCTIONS

Cut, Fold, and Press the Text Paper

1. Rough-cut 24 sheets of the interior paper to 6½" × 8¼" (16 × 21 cm).

2. Gently fold the entire stack of paper in half, bringing the 8¼" (21 cm) paper edges together. Hold them with both hands and try to have the edges fan evenly.

3. Bone them down.

4. Put the folded textblock under a weight for at least 4 hours or overnight.

Make a Jig and Trim the Textblock

5. Using scrap binder's or mat board, cut 1 piece that is at least the size of the textblock + 1" (2.5 cm) in height and width. In this model, we used a 7½" × 5" (19 × 12.5 cm) piece.

6. Cut 1 board the size of the final textblock: 6½" × 4" (16.5 × 10 cm).

7. Cut enough strips of board to 7½" × ¼" (19 cm × 6 mm) so that when they are stacked, they are equal to the thickness of the textblock + 1 board thickness (about ½" [1 cm]).

8. With double-sided tape or glue, adhere these strips to the long edge of the large board.

9. Cut enough strips of board to 5" × ¼" (12.5 cm × 6 mm) so that they equal the thickness of the textblock (about ½" [1.5 cm]).

10. Adhere these strips to the short side of the board. Make sure the walls of the jig are square. The textblock should be able to fit securely within the walls of the ¼" (6 mm) strips.

11. Fit the 6½" × 4" (16.5 × 10 cm) board on top of the textblock.

12. Holding the top board steady (use a small weight) make several slow cuts to the fore edge of the textblock. Use the top board as a guide to cut the fore edge so that all the pages are the same size.

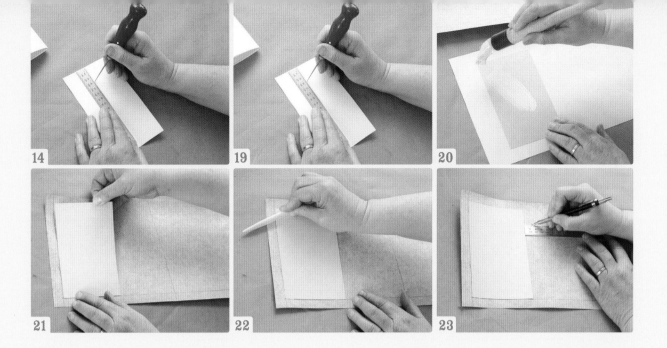

Make a Punching Template

13. Cut a waste piece of paper the length of the text-block (6½" [16.5 cm]) and about 2" (5 cm) wide.

14. Make a pair of marks for sewing stations at either end of the textblock. There should be 4 marks down the length of the waste paper at ¼" (6 mm), 1" (2.5 cm), 5" (12.5 cm), and 6" (15 cm). These will be the sewing stations.

Cut the Cover Materials

15. Cut 1 piece of book cloth to <u>12"</u> × 9" (<u>30.5</u> × 23 cm).

16. Cut 2 pieces of thin folder stock to the same size as the textblock, 6½" × 4" (<u>16.5</u> × 10 cm).

17. Cut 1 piece of book cloth for the spine piece the same length as the textblock and wide enough to overlap the sides somewhat: 6½" × 2" (<u>16.5</u> × 5 cm).

18. Cut 2 pieces of book cloth for the inside tabs, large enough to go just beyond the holes of the sewing stations and a bit on the interior of the textblock: 1" × 2" (2.5 × 5 cm). These protect the sewing but are *optional*.

Assemble the Cover

19. On the inside (glue side) of the book cloth, mark ¾" (2 cm) along the short edge for turn-ins and ¾" (2 cm) along the bottom edge. These are guide lines for cover placement.

20. On a piece of waste paper, glue out one of the covers.

21. Align the folder stock to the guide line you drew on the cloth.

22. Bone down the cover to adhere it to the folder stock.

23. From the edge of the cover that is farthest away from the edge of the cloth, measure ¾" (2 cm) away and draw a line. This is where the second cover will go. This measurement is the thickness of the textblock, plus the thickness of the covers.

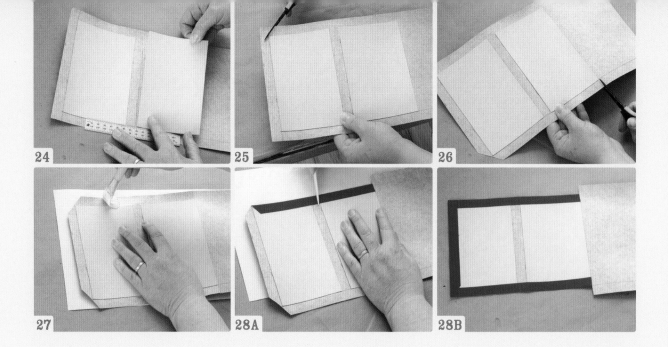

Assemble the Cover (continued)

24. On a piece of waste paper, glue out the second cover and align it to the guide marks on the cloth. Make sure the top and bottom edges of the covers are aligned.

25. Miter the 2 outside corners of the book cloth (the corners that are closest to the cloth edge), about 2 thicknesses of folder stock away from the corner of the front cover board.

26. Make a straight cut from the edge of the book cloth to the inside corners (the corners farthest away from cloth edge) of the back cover.

27. On a piece of waste paper, glue out the head and tail turn-ins of the cloth.

28. Fold them over and bone them down. Make sure the cloth is tight up against the edge of the boards. Work the single fore edge turn-in in the same manner.

Punch Holes for the Sewing Stations

29. On a scrap board or in a punching trough, starting at the middle, take a portion of the textblock and align the punching template within.

30. At the marks on the template, punch holes through the text paper. The holes do not need to be very large. Make sure the holes are right on the interior fold of the paper, not up on the sides.

31. Continue taking portions of the textblock and punching the sewing stations until you are finished. Keep the portions of the textblock in order.

32. Using the template, align the template within the center of the book cloth tabs, cloth side *up,* and punch the sewing stations.

33. Using the template, align the template within the center of the spine strip, cloth side *up,* and punch the sewing stations.

34. Using the template, align the template and the center space between the covers and punch the sewing stations.

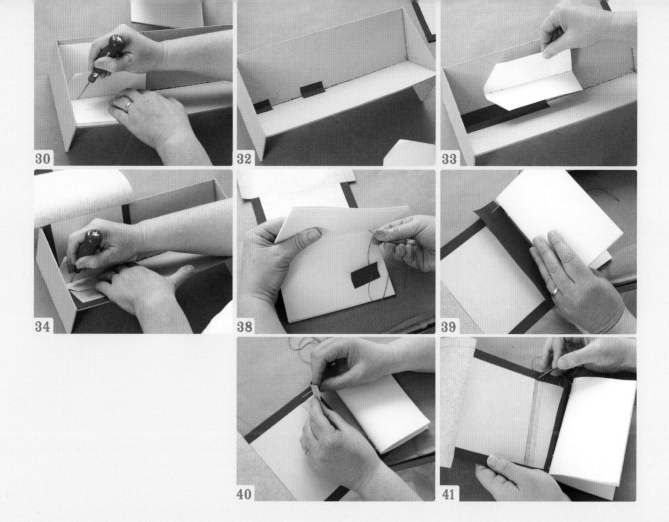

Sew the Book

35. Choose an appropriate color of 18/3 unwaxed linen thread, about 12" (30 cm) in length. Thread the needle.

36. The thread can go in either the inside or the outside of the textblock, depending on where the knot will show.

37. For the knot on the inside, start from the inside of the textblock, keeping all the pieces aligned in their place. All the prepunched holes should be lined up.

38. Bring the thread through one of the tabs (glue side down), through the hole that was punched, nearest to the edge. Leave a length of thread about 1½" (4 cm) long on the inside of the textblock.

39. Bring the thread through the textblock, and through the hole.

40. Bring the thread through the spine piece (glue side down), and through the hole.

41. Bring the thread through the spine of the cover, and through the hole.

42A   42B   43

44   45   46

Sew the Book (continued)

42. Bring the thread over to the second hole (at 1" [2.5 cm]). Go through the holes in the stack of materials until the needle is on the inside.

43. Tie a square knot with the length of thread. Cut the thread to a short length, about ¾" (2 cm).

44. Proceed to the second sewing station, and repeat steps 35 through 43.

> **TIP**   **Decoration Opportunity!**
>
> Add some beads to your stitches.

Glue the Spine Strip

45. With a piece of waste paper under one side of the spine strip, gently glue out the back of the book cloth. Leave the very center without glue.

46. Adhere the book cloth to the cover and bone it down.

47. Repeat steps 45 and 46 for the other side of the spine strip.

Make the Front Pocket

48. On a thicker piece of paper approximately 7" × 8¼" (17.5 × 21 cm), measure ¼" (6 mm) from the left edge of the paper inward. Mark and score that line with the bone folder and a 90-degree triangle or ruler.

49. Measure ½" (1.5 cm) from the bottom of the paper inward. Mark and score that line with the bone folder.

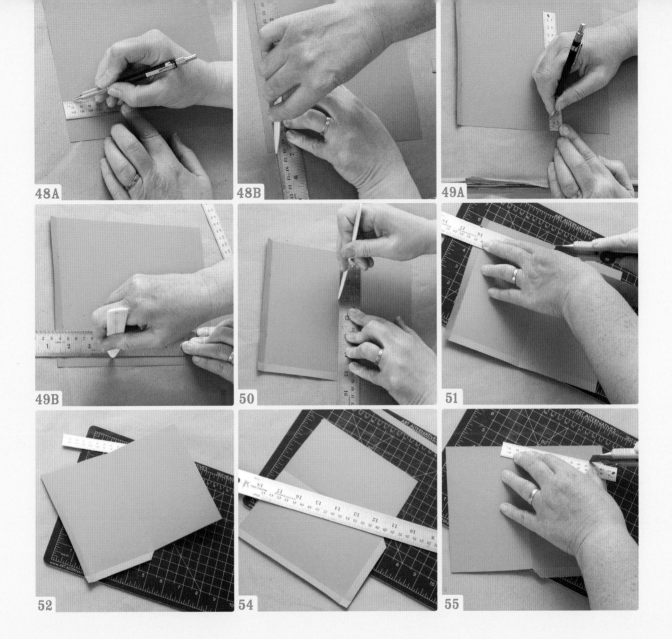

48A 48B 49A

49B 50 51

52 54 55

50. Measure, mark, and score 1 line 3¾" (9.5 cm) from the left score **or** 4" (10 cm) from the left edge.

51. Measure and mark a line 6¼" (16 cm) from the bottom score **or** 6½" (16.5 cm) from the bottom edge. Trim to this line; it is the length of the pocket.

52. You have created two tabs that will secure the back of the pocket. The left side of the paper is the front of the pocket. The right side is the back.

53. The back folds over and two of the tabs you created will hold it in place. The back will need to fit into the front piece, so it will need to be trimmed to a size slightly smaller than the front.

54. Trim the length of the back panel to 6" (15 cm). Angle the bottom cut slightly so that it fits into the bottom tab and lays flat.

55. Slightly miter the top of the pocket. Angle the cut from the fold down, approximately ¾" (2 cm).

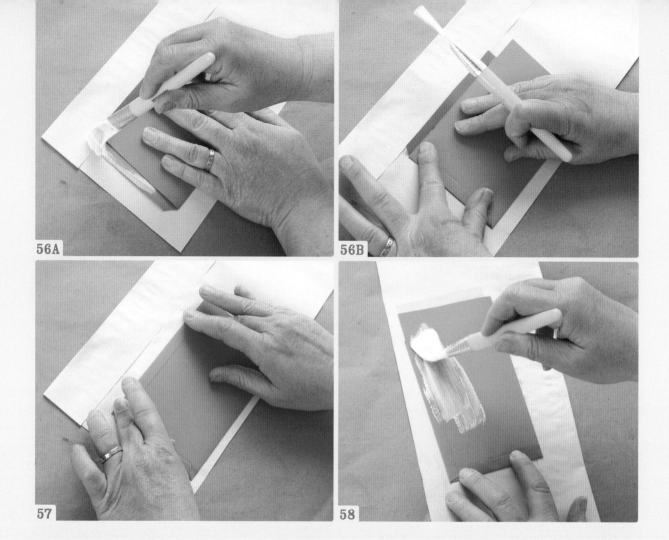

56A

56B

57

58

Assemble the Pocket

56. On a piece of waste paper, glue the bottom tab. Fold the back panel in and adhere the tab.

57. On a piece of waste paper, glue out the side tab and adhere it to the back panel.

Attach the Pocket

58. Insert a scrap piece of folder stock (6¾" × 3½" [17 x 9 cm]) into the pocket. Glue the back of the pocket.

59. Align the pocket on the inside of the front cover.

60. Bone down the pocket. Turn the book over and bone down the pocket from the back.

61. Put a board and a weight on the pocket and let it dry.

Make the Closure Flap

62. Fold the extra book cloth along the back at 2½" (6.5 cm) so that it overlaps about ¾" (2 cm) over the back cover. This will cover the edge of the back cover.

63. Holding the pen in place, see how the back flap looks when the book is closed. Should the flap be shorter? If there is too much material, mark and cut off the excess at 6" (15 cm).

59

60

62

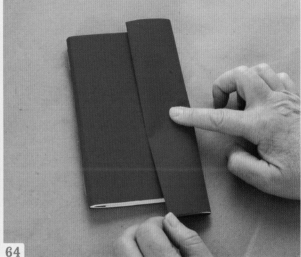

64

Make the Closure

64. On the extra book cloth, decide where the button closure should be (at 3¼" [8 cm], it should be in the middle of the length of the board and ½" [1.5 cm] down from the fold).

65. Mark that spot.

66. Sew the button onto the extra fabric that will be the flap.

66

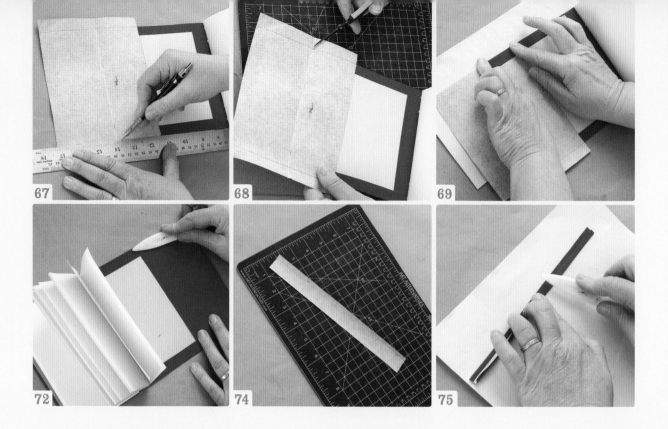

Adhere the Back Flap

The material that becomes the back flap is about 1½× the width of the textblock. The fold of the book cloth has to cover the inside of the flap, the sewing for the button, and the edge of the back cover.

67. Measure and mark the turn-in for 3" (7.5 cm) of the extra book cloth (that is, up to the fold that makes the flap).

68. Make an angled cut where the turn-in will end.

69. Glue the turn-in, fold it down, and bone it over.

70. Trim the remaining edge of the flap material so that when it is glued down, the edges of the material are inside the border of the turn-ins.

71. The end of the material should overlap the back cover by about ½" (1.5 cm).

72. Glue out the material and rub it down well with the bone folder.

Make a Pen Loop

73. Cut a strip of the heavier paper to 1" × 4" (2.5 × 10 cm).

74. Measure, mark, and score ¼" (6 mm) for either edge so that when folded, the long edges meet down the center.

75. On a piece of waste paper, glue out, fold, and bone down the paper.

76. Wrap the paper strip around the pen.

77. Align the pen so that it sits just at the edge of the textblock on the back cover; mark that spot.

78. Trim the pen loop to a size that will encompass the pen as well as allow for material to be glued down, about 2" (5 cm).

79. Glue the ends of the loop together.

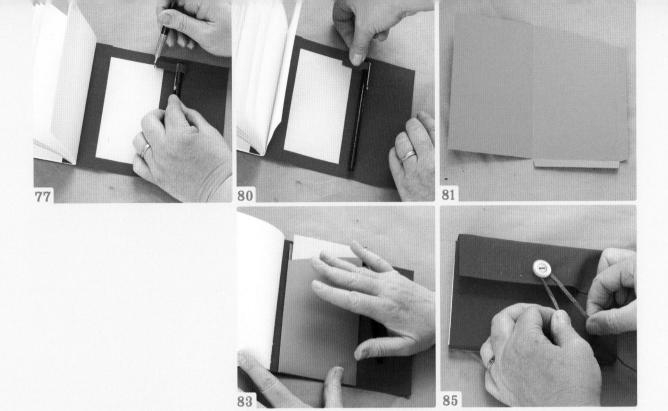

Make the Back Pocket

80. Glue the loop to the back cover, where it will fit along the edge of the textblock but will not interfere with closing the book.

Make the Back Pocket

The back pocket is almost a mirror image of the front pocket.

81. As in the front pocket, slightly angle the bottom edge of the back panel, and trim the edge of the back panel so that it fits smoothly within the front panel tabs.

82. After trimming the back panel, fold over the back panel and adhere the bottom and side tabs with glue to secure.

83. Crease the back panel at the top of the front of the pocket (6" [15 cm]). Adhere the back pocket over the pen loop and bone it down.

Add a Ribbon to Close

84. Cut a piece of ribbon 10" (25.5 cm) in length.

85. Tie one end of the ribbon under the button.

86. To close, fold the book, wrap the flap around the front of the book, wrap the ribbon around the entire item, and secure it to the button.

87. Keep it folded until it is dry.

Book in a Box

STUDIO PROJECT

Make a delightful, self-contained book box. For this project, you will create a box around the front cover of a premade book. You can add walls to the sides of either a commercially bound book or a hand-bound book. The edges and content will be protected while allowing ease of use. The Book in a Box also serves a dual purpose by containing any materials that may have a tendency to fall out.

SIZE
Custom

TIME
Time: approx. 1½ hours
Prep: 20 minutes
Make: 1 hour
Downtime/Drying time: Preferably overnight

The materials required include decorative paper, glue, thread, binder's board, textblock, board papers, book cloth, hand drill, and ruler.

TOOLS
- Bone folder
- Glue brush
- Knife
- Weights

MATERIALS
- Book cloth
- Decorative paper
- Binder's board
- A hardcover book with a rounded spine
- PVA
- .010 pt. board

INSTRUCTIONS

Measure the Book

1. Measure the thickness of the book, including the covers.

2. Measure the height and width of the book.

Cut the Materials

The head and tail pieces will be the width of the book, with a rounded end to mirror the rounded spine of a premade book.

3. Cut a strip of binder's board to the thickness of the book and 2× the width + the height of the book. Alternatively, cut 3 pieces of board: 2 pieces the thickness of the book x the width, plus a bit (about ¼" [6 mm]), and 1 piece the thickness of the book × the height.

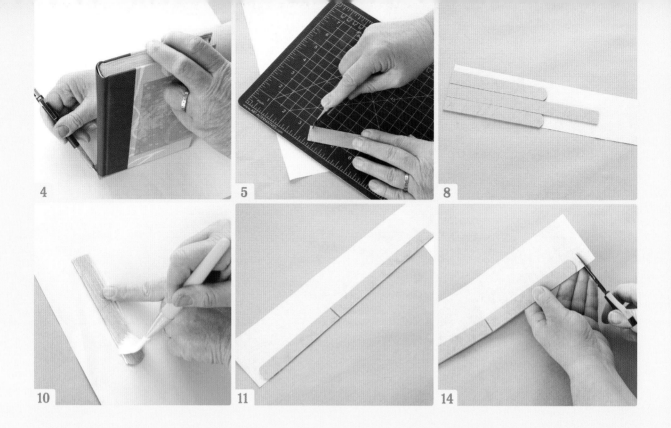

Cut the Materials (continued)

4. Place the tail of the book flat on the binder's board strip with the spine edge facing in. Trace around the spine edge of the book to mark the round of the spine.

5. Carefully cut the shape of the spine.

6. Use the cut piece as a template to trace around and cut a second piece with the same round.

7. Cut a strip of binder's board to the height of the book.

Cover the Box Walls

8. Cut a strip of book cloth to 3½× the height of the binders board strips and 2× the width + the height + 1" (2.5 cm).

9. Determine the alignment of the walls along the edge of the cloth. The short sides are at the end with the rounded end facing out. The distance between the boards is one board thickness.

10. Glue out one of the side walls. Place it on the cloth strip along the bottom edge of the cloth, with a turn-in of cloth at the end of about ¼" (6 mm).

11. Glue out the center or book height board and place it one board thickness away from the side wall on the cloth, also along the edge of the cloth.

12. Glue out the second wall and place it one board thickness away from the center board with the round edge facing out, placing it along the edge of the cloth.

13. Bone it down.

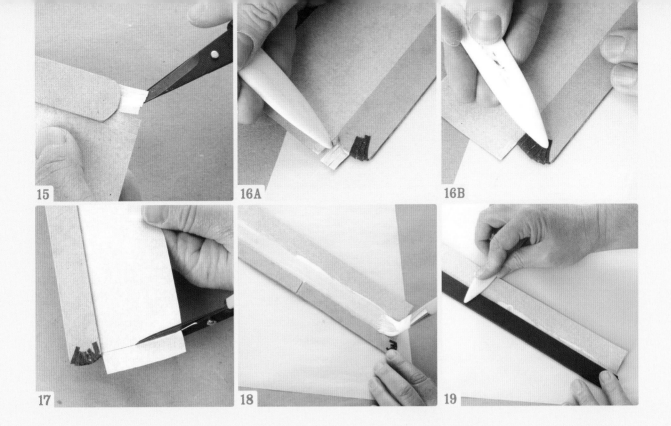

Trim and Glue for the Round Spine

Covering a round edge is easier when the covering material is cut into small tabs that can be molded around the nonsquare edge.

14. Carefully trim back the excess book cloth on the end, only along the spine round. Trim it to about ½" (1.5 cm).

15. Make a series of straight cuts from the edge of the cloth to the edge of the board. As the small tabs fold over the round edge, they will bend and overlap, covering the edge of the board.

16. Glue the tabs out and glue them down to the binder's board, being sure to work them into place with a bone folder.

17. Trim the extra cloth at the ends of the cloth strip. This extra cloth would be larger than the rounded end of the wall.

18. Glue out enough of the cloth to adhere one side of the wall.

19. Roll the book cloth around the already adhered pieces of binder's board and bone it down. The cloth will wrap around the binder's board wall three times, to make sure all of the surfaces are covered and no binder's board can be seen.

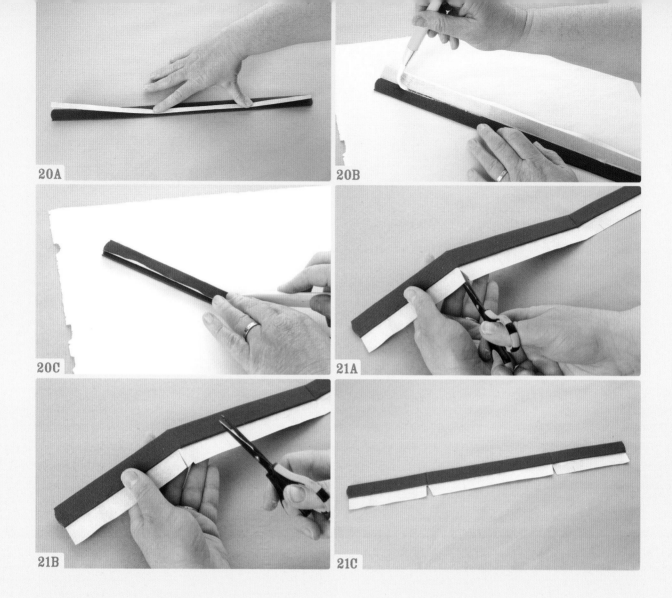

20A

20B

20C

21A

21B

21C

Trim and Glue for the
Round Spine (continued)

20. Continue to wrap the book cloth around the boards, stopping one board thickness from the edge of the board on the third wrap.

21. Carefully trim out the book cloth "corners" where the cloth abuts the one board thickness space between the boards.

Glue onto the Book

22. Gingerly apply a line of glue along the back edges of the book. It is not necessary to use a lot of glue.

23. Beginning from the center, and using a low-tack tape if need be, attach the cloth-covered board to the fore edge of the front cover of the book, and then carefully work it along the head and the tail.

24. Glue the interior tabs down to the inside front cover of the book.

25. Use weights to keep the walls erect and the book open while it dries.

Cover the Back Turn-ins

26. Cut a piece of paper to the size of the inside of the box or use the fly leaf from the book.

27. Carefully glue it out and adhere it in the back of the book, being sure to bone it down evenly.

28. Place a fence of .010 pt. board on top of the wet paper and close the book.

29. Let it dry under a weight.

The Book Artist's
Gallery

You can do a lot of different things now that you've mastered the techniques in this book. Here are some variations on some of the projects we've featured. What will you do with your book?

Limp Paper, Amy Lapidow.
Background: print by Margaret Langdell.
Foreground: support tapes spell out BOOKS and PAPER in Morse code.

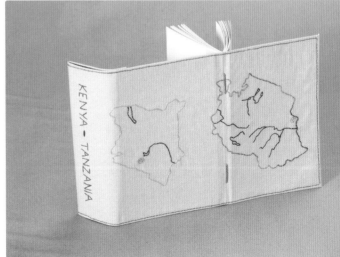

Travel Journal, Embroidered book cloth, Sarah Hulsey.

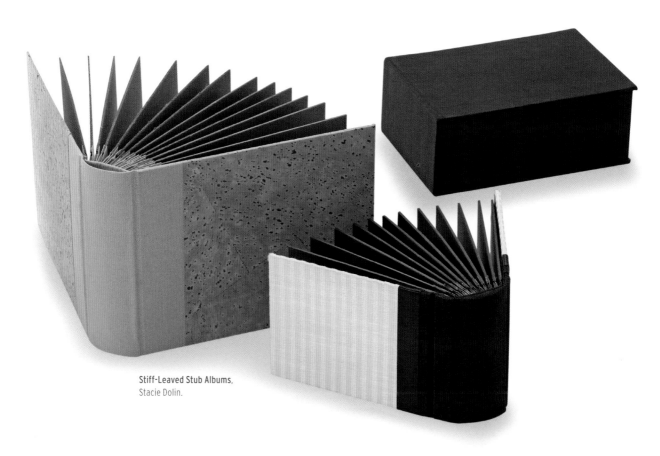

Stiff-Leaved Stub Albums,
Stacie Dolin.

Friend-of-a-Friend Book, Stacie Dolin.
Covered in cork

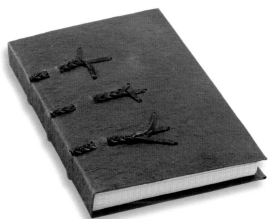

Limp Paper, Stacie Dolin.
Handmade paper: by Cave Paper.
Supports of braided leather

Stiff-Leaved Stub Album, McKey Berkman.

Woven Albums, Amy Lapidow.
Background: handmade paper leaves
Foreground: watercolor paper with
painted Tyvek covers and laces

Tacketed Book with French Box, Amy Lapidow.

Book in a Slipcase in a French Box in a Clamshell Box, McKey Berkman.

Friend-of-a-Friend Book with traditional marbled paper, Barbara Halporn.

Travel Journals, Amy Lapidow.
Background: painted Tyvek covers,
expandable pocket with Mylar and flap
Foreground: tab closure; foreground bottom
fabric backed with interfacing

FIGURING
WOMEN

Accordian Album with Frames, Todd Pattison.

Accordian Album with Frames, Stacie Dolin.
Paper cutouts in accordion structure as a
tunnel book

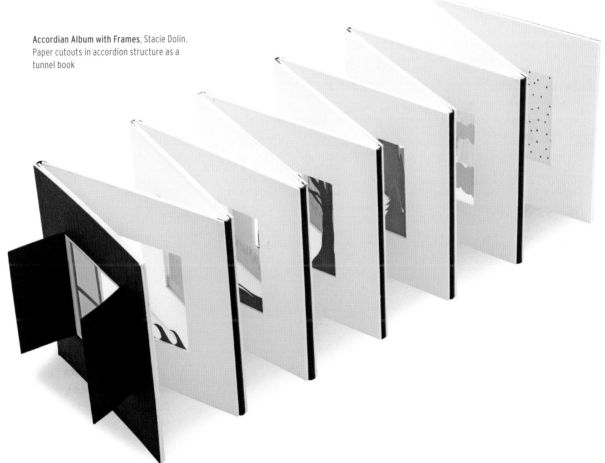

Resources

Contributors

Barbara Halporn
McKey Berkman
Sarah Hulsey
Todd Pattison

Further Reading

Fox, Gabrielle
Essential Guide to Making Handmade Books
North Light Books, 2000
ISBN: 1-58180-019-3

Frost, Gary
Sewn Board Books
The Ampersand, 1991, p. 5

Golden, Alisa
Creating Handmade Books
Sterling, 1998;
ISBN: 978-0-80691-771-7
Unique Handmade Books
Sterling, 2001
ISBN: 0-8069-5813-8

Grant, Richard
About Paper Grain
Skin Deep, Volume 10,
Autumn 2000
www.hewit.com/skin_deep/?
volume=10&article=1#article

Moote, Cheryl
www.mootepoints.com
Simply Bound, 2001
Slight of Binding, 2002
Books with Girth, 2005

Smith, Esther
How to Make Books
Potter Craft, 2007
ISBN: 978-0-30735-336-8

Stein, Jeannine
Re-Bound
Quarry Books, 2009
ISBN: 978-1-59253-524-8

Thompson, Jason
Playing with Books
Quarry Books, 2010
ISBN: 978-59523-600-9

Withers, Laurence
How to Fold
Pepin Press, 2005
ISBN: 978-9-05768-039-4

Zeier, Franz
Books, Boxes, and Portfolios
Design Press, 1990
ISBN: 0-8306-3483-5

Resources for Bookbinding Supplies

American Science and Surplus
P.O. Box 1030
Skokie, IL 60076
847.647.0011
www.sciplus.com
All manner of surplus materials. Good resource for tape, scalpels, and assorted tools.

BoneFolder.com
146 Halstead St.
Rochester, NY 14610
585.482.7870
www.bonefolder.com
All kinds of Teflon tools

Bookmakers
8601 Rhode Island Ave.
College Park, MD 20740
301.345.7979
www.bookmakerscatalog.com
All manner of bookbinding supplies

C-Thru Ruler
6 Britton Drive
Bloomfield, CT 06002
800.243.0303
www.cthruruler.com
Gridded triangles with cutting edge

HamiltonBook.com
www.hamiltonbook.com
Discount and remaindered books on all subjects

Ernst Schaefer
731 Lehigh Ave.
Union, NJ 07083
908.964.280
www.ernestschaeferinc.com
Good source for binder's board

Hewitt and Sons
12 Wettlehill Road
Houston Industrial Estate
Livington, West Lothian
EH54 52L Scotland
www.hewittsonline.com
General bookbinding supplies

John Neal Booksellers
1833 Spring Garden St.
Greensboro, NC 27403
800.369.9598
www.johnnealbooks.com
*Books and supplies for
bookbinding and calligraphy*

Kutrimmer
www.kutrimmer.com
*Paper cutters suitable for
bookbinding*

Limited Paper
Industry City Better Papers LLC
67 34th St., 4th Floor
Brooklyn, NY 11232
800.797.7022
www.limitedpapers.com
A wide variety of text papers

New York Central Art Supply
62 Third Ave.
New York, NY 10003
800.950.6111
www.nycentralartsupply.com
*Extensive paper selection.
Ask for the paper department
or the paper catalogue. Very
knowledgeable staff.*

Paper Mojo
7711 Welborn St., Suite 105
Raleigh, NC 27615
800.428.3818
www.papermojo.com
*A wide variety of decorative
papers*

Shepherds
76 Southampton Row
London WCIB 4AR, England
www.bookbinding.co.uk
General bookbinding supplies

Starrett Tools
www.starrett.com
*Precision tools of all kinds. Avail-
able through distributors only.*

Talas
330 Morgan Ave.
Brooklyn, NY 11211
212.219.0770
www.talasonline.com
General bookbinding supplies

Thread Needle Street
485 Front St. North, Suite B
Issaquah, WA 98027
425. 391.0528
www.threadneedlestreet.com
*Linen and silk threads in many
colors and sizes*

Organizations

The Guild of Bookworkers
521 Fifth Ave.
New York, NY 10175-0038
www.guildofbookworkers.org

**Canadian Bookbinders and
Book Artists Guild**
C B B A G
80 Ward St., Suite 207
Toronto, Ontario
Canada M6H 4A6
416.581.1071
www.cbbag.ca

College Book Arts Association
www.collegebookart.org

Society of Bookbinders (UK)
www.societyofbookbinders.com

The BookartsWeb
www.philobiblon.com
*A portal to much bookbinding
information*

About the Authors

Stacie Dolin is a bookbinder and consummate crafter located in Arlington, Massachusetts. After working in the silkscreen industry for a number of years, she moved to Boston to study bookbinding at the North Bennet Street School. She now teaches numerous bookbinding workshops and does independent binding and book repair. When not playing with books, Stacie knits, spins, and quilts, and looks for ways to integrate her fiber activities into her bookbinding. To see more of her work, go to www.posthornpublishing.blogspot.com

Amy Lapidow is a hand bookbinder, trained at the North Bennet Street School and several other institutions including Rare Book School and CBBAG. She teaches through the NBSS workshop program, where she has developed classes on a number of bookbinding concepts. Her personal interest is taking historic bookbinding structures and updating them by using alternate materials for contemporary uses. Her work has been seen in *500 Handmade Books* and as part of the exhibit *One Book Many Interpretations* at the Chicago Public Library, where she combined a classic binding style with QR codes. She lives in Somerville, Massachusetts. See more of her work at www.thethreeringbinders.com.

Acknowledgments

We would like to thank:

- Tiffany Hill for the opportunity to write this book, and for all her help in getting it done.
- David Martinell and Glenn Scott for making the books look so good.
- Charlie for carrying heavy things.
- Our students, so we knew how to approach this project.
- The Binders at 11 Miller Street, for their patience, support, and contributions—John O'Regan, McKey Berkman, Sarah Hulsey, Barbara Halporn, Dana Kull, and Kate Rich

Amy's special thank you to:

- Stacie, so I did not have to do this alone.
- The North Bennet Street School for my training and teaching experience.
- My teachers, Mark Esser and Sally Key, who showed me the way.

Stacie would like to especially thank:

- Amy, for inviting me to join her on this journey.
- My family, for encouraging me to be crafty.

Index

Further Reading from Quarry Books

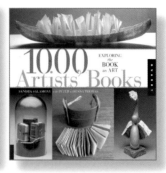

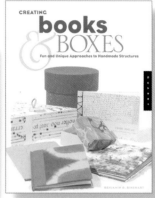

Playing with Books
978-1-59253-600-9

Re-Bound
978-1-59253-524-8

1,000 Artists' Books
978-1-59253-774-7

Creating Books & Boxes
978-1-59253-291-9

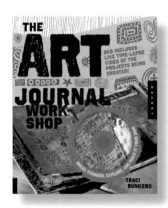

The Art Journal Workshop
978-1-59253-684-9

Painted Pages
978-1-59253-686-3

Cultivating Your Creative Life
978-1-59253-786-0

Playing with Paper
978-1-59253-814-0